An American Annual
of Christmas Literature
and Art

Christmas

HIS NAME shall be called Wonderful, Counsellor, the Mighty God, the Everlasting Father, the Prince of Peace

ISAIAH 9:6

Volume 50

An American Annual
of Christmas Literature
and Art

Edited by Randolph E. Haugan
Augsburg Publishing House
Publishers · Minneapolis

Christmas

Table of Contents

Volume Fifty

First Edition

Nineteen Hundred Eighty

Acknowledgments

SIMEON
Illustration by Betty Sievert

SONG FOR SIMEON
Illustration by Audrey Teeple

A PENNY FOR A MIRACLE
Stamps for photographs courtesy of Agnes Harrigan Mueller, Virginia Haywood,
and the American Lung Association

VICTORIAN TOYS
Dolls for photographs courtesy of Audrey Teeple

CHRISTMAS CAPER
Illustrations by Melva Mickelson

CHRISTMAS MUSIC
Calligraphy by Hildegard Szendrey
Illustrations by Audrey Teeple

CHRISTMAS AT ST. OLAF
Photos courtesy of St. Olaf College

CHRISTMAS HAS A SECRET
Illustration by Melva Mickelson

MANUSCRIPT EDITOR: Karen Walhof

MUSIC EDITOR: Allan Mahnke

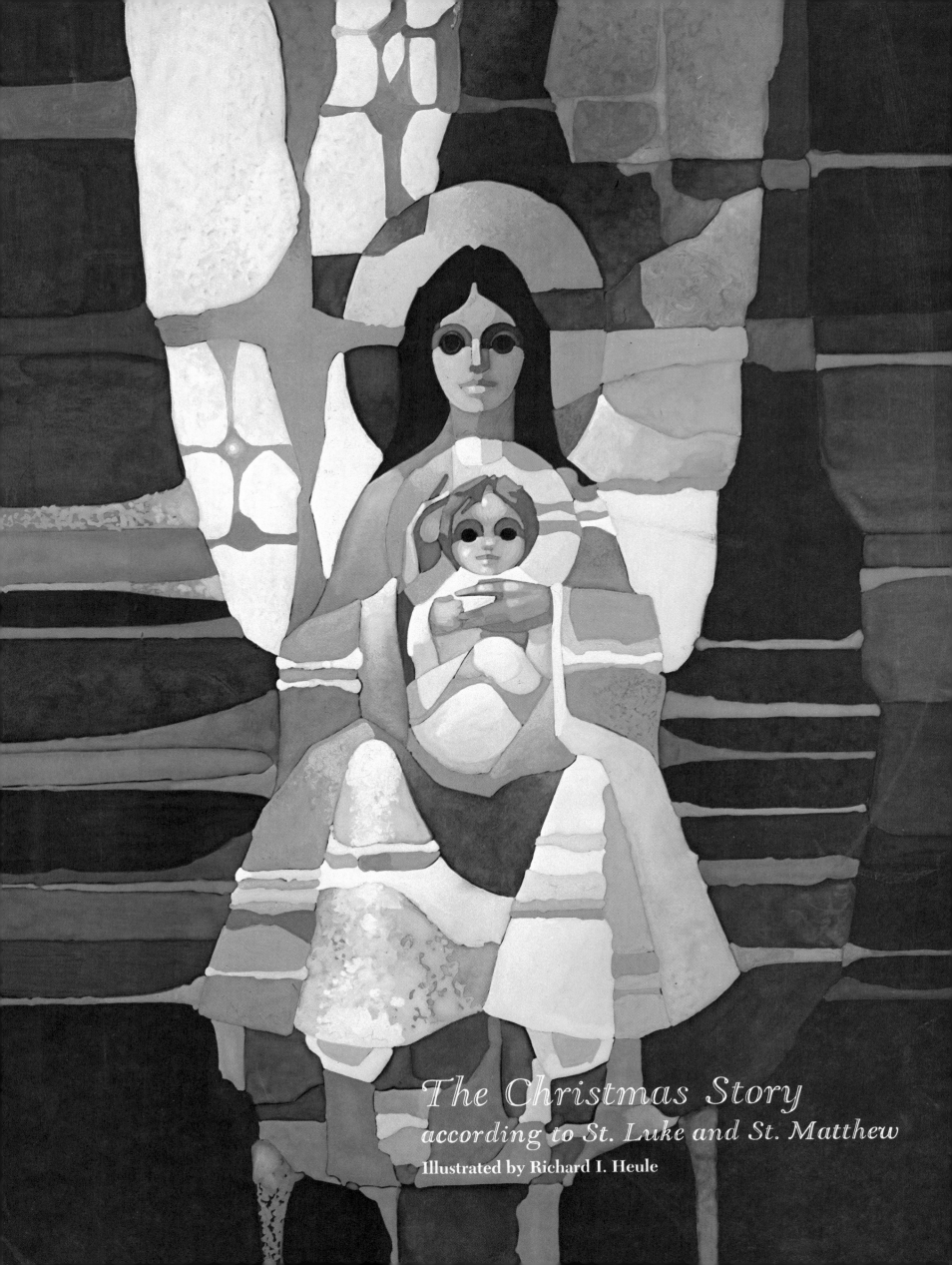

The Christmas Story
according to St. Luke and St. Matthew
Illustrated by Richard I. Heule

And it came to pass in those days, that there went out a decree from Caesar Augustus, that all the world should be taxed. (And this taxing was first made when Cyrenius was governor of Syria.) And all went to be taxed, every one into his own city. And Joseph also went up from Galilee, out of the city of Nazareth, into Judaea, unto the city of David, which is called Bethlehem; (because he was of the house and lineage of David:) To be taxed with Mary his espoused wife, being great with child. And so it was, that, while they were there, the days were accomplished that she should be delivered. And she brought forth her firstborn son, and wrapped him in swaddling clothes, and laid him in a manger; because there was no room for them in the inn. And there were in the same country shepherds abiding in the field, keeping watch over their flock by night. And, lo, the angel of the Lord came upon them, and the glory of the Lord shone round about them: and they were sore afraid.

And the angel said unto them, Fear not:
for, behold, I bring you good tidings of great joy, which shall be to all people. For unto you is born this day in the city of David a Saviour, which is Christ the Lord. And this shall be a sign unto you; Ye shall find the babe wrapped in swaddling clothes, lying in a manger. And suddenly there was with the angel a multitude of the heavenly host praising God, and saying, Glory to God in the highest, and on earth peace, good will toward men. And it came to pass, as the angels were gone away from them into heaven, the shepherds said one to another, Let us now go even unto Bethlehem, and see this thing which is come to pass, which the Lord hath made known unto us. And they came with haste, and found Mary, and Joseph, and the babe lying in a manger. And when they had seen it, they made known abroad the saying which was told them concerning this child. And all they that heard it wondered at those things which were told them by the shepherds. But Mary kept all these things, and pondered them in her heart. And the shepherds returned, glorifying and praising God for all the things that they had heard and seen, as it was told unto them.

Now when Jesus was born in Bethlehem

of Judaea in the days of Herod the king, behold,
there came wise men from the east to Jerusalem,
saying, Where is he that is born King of the Jews?
for we have seen his star in the east, and are come to
worship him. When Herod the king had heard these
things, he was troubled, and all Jerusalem with him.
And when he had gathered all the chief priests and
scribes of the people together, he demanded of them
where Christ should be born. And they said unto him,
In Bethlehem of Judaea: for thus it is written by the
prophet, And thou Bethlehem, in the land of Juda,
art not the least among the princes of Juda: for out
of thee shall come a Governor, that shall rule my
people Israel. Then Herod, when he had privily
called the wise men, enquired of them diligently
what time the star appeared. And he sent them to
Bethlehem, and said, Go and search diligently for
the young child; and when ye have found him, bring
me word again, that I may come and worship him also.
When they had heard the king, they departed; and,
lo, the star, which they saw in the east, went before
them, till it came and stood over where the young
child was. When they saw the star, they rejoiced
with exceeding great joy. And when they were come
into the house, they saw the young child with Mary
his mother, and fell down, and worshipped him: and
when they had opened their treasures, they presented
unto him gifts; gold, and frankincense, and myrrh.
And being warned of God in a dream that they
should not return to Herod, they departed
into their own country another way.

And when they were departed, behold,
the angel of the Lord appeareth to Joseph in a
dream, saying, Arise, and take the young child and
his mother, and flee into Egypt, and be thou there
until I bring thee word: for Herod will seek the young
child to destroy him. When he arose, he took the
young child and his mother by night, and departed
into Egypt: And was there until the death of Herod:
that it might be fulfilled which was spoken of the
Lord by the prophet, saying, Out of Egypt have I
called my son. . . . But when Herod was dead,
behold, an angel of the Lord appeareth in a dream
to Joseph in Egypt, saying, Arise, and take the young
child and his mother, and go into the land of Israel:
for they are dead which sought the young child's life.
And he arose, and took the young child and his
mother, and came into the land of Israel.

"... for mine eyes have seen thy salvation ..."

Simeon

ALVIN N. ROGNESS

JOSEPH AND MARY'S unexpected encounter with Simeon in the temple wasn't the first time they had occasion to wonder. It began with the angel's visit to Mary long before. This Jesus was not to be an ordinary child, or man. Elizabeth's cry, "Blessed are you among women, and blessed is the fruit of your womb," reinforced Mary's growing awareness that her child would be unique in the world. Then came the decree from Caesar Augustus which brought Mary to Bethlehem for the birth, as the prophets had foretold. There, at Bethlehem, her mind was awhirl with wonder—the shepherds reporting the song of the angels, the Wise Men from the East following a star, and later the vision which sent Joseph and Mary to Egypt in safe exile from the fury of Herod.

But now they met the aged Simeon. Earlier, on the eighth day, Jesus had been circumcised and formally given the name Jesus, the name assigned to him by the angel at the visitation. It was now 80 days after the birth of their firstborn, and Joseph and Mary, following tradition, dutifully came to the temple in Jerusalem for the customary rites of the mother's purification, prescribed by the law of Moses.

On this day Simeon had been strangely moved to go to the temple. Immediately upon seeing Jesus and his parents, Simeon knew that his longings and yearn-ings (and the expectations of his people, Israel) were fulfilled. This was the Messiah, the Savior not just of Israel but of all the world. He reached out and took him tenderly into his arms, and spoke those words which have become a cherished part of the liturgies of Christendom, the Nunc Dimittis:

Lord, now lettest thou thy servant depart in
    peace, according to thy word;
for mine eyes have seen thy salvation
which thou hast prepared in the presence of
    all peoples,
a light for revelation to the Gentiles,
and for glory to thy people Israel.

With that he blessed them, and said to Mary his mother,

Behold, this child is set for the fall and
    rising of many in Israel,
and for a sign that is spoken against
(and a sword will pierce through your own soul also),
that thoughts out of many hearts may be revealed.

This is Simeon's only appearance. Tradition says that he was the son of Hillel, and the father of Gama-liel, the celebrated teacher of Paul. Luke describes him as "righteous and devout, looking for the consolation of Israel, and the Holy Spirit was upon him." Furthermore, according to Luke, his appearance in the temple was not a coincidence. It had been revealed to him by the Spirit that he would not die before he had seen the Messiah—and this was the day.

Like other devout Israelites who had clung to the promises of a Messiah, he probably thought primarily in terms of someone who would restore the ancient glory of the nation. Nor was this strange. For centuries this tiny country had been buffeted by a parade of powerful countries. Again and again, they had been captured and, as often happened in those days, the people had been taken from their land to be slaves and servants in the conquering countries. Again and again, a remnant had returned to Palestine to rebuild and reclaim the promises given to Abraham and Moses. Even the disciples themselves, after being with Jesus day after day, harbored such hopes; bewildered, they scattered that tragic Friday when Christ was crucified. Not until after the resurrection did they begin to understand the worldwide salvation which Jesus had come to bring.

THERE IS a clue in Simeon's cryptic rhapsody, however: "a light for revelation to the Gentiles." In his words, if not in his comprehension at the moment, was couched the staggering dimensions of the Messiah's mission. Jesus was a Jew, born of a Jewish mother, reared in the faith of Israel; both he and his family were devoutly faithful to their traditions and practices. But this was merely the launching pad for his mission to the world. God had designed it to be that from the time he chose Abraham and his family to set the stage for the invasion of the world by his only Son.

It was not the first time Mary had pondered the place of her son. The angel had told her that he would be great and be called "the Son of the Most High." With the promise that he would be given the throne of "his father David," she too probably thought of him as becoming a great leader of the nation. With the Wise Men coming from the East to worship him, she must have wondered what more would be in store for him. And now, with the words of Simeon about the Gentiles, she had new reason to puzzle over the future of her firstborn.

Only one other incident reveals Mary's continuing wonder. When Jesus was 12 years old, his parents brought him to Jerusalem for the festival of the Passover. When they did not find him among friends on the return journey to Nazareth, they returned to Jerusalem to find him in the temple, where he said, "Did you not know that I must be in my Father's house?" Luke adds, "and his mother kept all these things in her heart."

How long Mary lived and how much of his mission she was given to understand before she died, we do not know. We know she was there at his crucifixion, and that she knew of his resurrection. Doubtless she was among the followers on that eventful Pentecost when the Holy Spirit was given. And she may have lived long enough to see the disciples scatter to bring the gospel to the world.

He had given the marching orders, "Go . . . make disciples of all nations." It seems almost incredible that a few unlettered followers should take this staggering demand seriously. But they did, and before the first century had ended, cells of Christianity had sprouted in almost every major center of the Roman Empire. Who, even then, could have envisaged the church of today? Among all the religions by which people seek to worship, Christianity is the most widely spread, embraces the largest number of adherents, and makes the most stupendous claims for the divinity of its founder and the finality of its teachings—it counts one out of every four people on earth in its membership. The prophesy of Simeon amazingly has been fulfilled.

Simeon had warned Mary that "a sword will pierce through your own soul also." There was suffering for her. There was the sadness of never quite being able to understand this son who, though fully human, obviously wore a different mantle. There were times when he seemed to reject her. And to stand at the cross, as she did, to see her own son writhe to his death—this must indeed have been soul-piercing.

Nor is Jesus the source of both sorrow and joy for Mary alone. He is the decisive figure of history. To reject him or to live apart from him is to live in the sorrow of guilt, of meaninglessness, and of hopelessness. To live with him is the key to the profoundest joys of earth. He is set indeed "for the fall and rising of many."

ALMOST 2000 years have gone by since Simeon peered into the future and glimpsed the worldwide role of Jesus. During these centuries, and even today, there is no figure that so dominates history. It is impossible to array him with other great leaders. He belongs in no pantheon. He stands alone, even measured by secular standards. He has enlisted the loyalty of more hundreds of millions than all the kings and emperors put together. Other world leaders, upon death, retreat to quiet places on library shelves, but not Jesus. He walks the paths of men. He steals quietly into their hearts. He stirs their wills to an obedience given none other.

Simeon was looking for the "consolation of Israel." He was looking for a time when his people would know comfort and hope and peace. These are the gifts of the kingdom which Jesus came to bring. They will not always find political expression, perhaps rarely so. But in the midst of suffering and even catastrophe, people who have come to Jesus for the forgiveness of their sins and for their restored rights as sons and daughters of the heavenly Father—for them the consolation is real. In many parts of the world today the political conditions yield little comfort or hope or peace. But in every land there are people who live and work in the maelstrom of threatening dangers, and yet have courage and hope. They know the bracing consolation of an eternal kingdom.

Not everyone in Simeon's day lived in expectation of the coming Messiah. Perhaps only a few. The prophets had foretold his coming again and again, but he had not come. Meanwhile Israel was in continuous political bondage, at that time under the heel of Rome. King Herod and the religious leaders had learned to accommodate themselves to the oppressor, collecting his taxes and suppressing any uprising. The promise, or threat, of a Messiah frightened them. What leader could match the power of Rome? Any attempt for freedom could only bring bloody reprisal. When Jesus appeared as a possible leader, they plotted his death with the sensible logic that it was better that one man die than that a whole people perish.

THE SHEPHERDS on the hillside that Bethlehem night must have taken seriously the promise of a coming Messiah. The appearance of the angel frightened them, but the great message—"I bring you good news of a great joy which will come to all the people; for to you is born this day in the city of David a Savior, who is Christ the Lord"—sent them in exultant search of the child. And God must have put into the longings and yearnings of the Wise Men from the East this same expectation.

In every age there are believers who look into the future with confidence and hope that the Lord will come. Not only will he come on the last day in glory, but in the midst of life's sins and sorrows, temptations and tragedies he comes. These are the people who, like Simeon, live close to the Word, who rely with

almost childlike naivete on the explicit promises of the Lord. And Scripture is full of such reassurance. Full into the face of our fears, Christ tells us that he has overcome the world, that it is the Father's good pleasure to give us the kingdom, that if we seek this kingdom all needful things will be added, that he will be with us to the end of the age, and that he has gone on to prepare a place for us in the eternal home.

We can be certain of this: It was no easier for Simeon to believe in the promises than for us. Life was grim in the first century. It had been grim in Egypt when God sent Moses to lead his people out of the grinding slavery of Pharaoh. It had been grim when one tyrant after another swept them into new bondage. And in the centuries since Simeon the world has never become so good that people's hopes could soar.

The twentieth century is no exception. The massive, complex issues that face our shrunken world loom dark on the horizon. For the first time in history, we wonder whether the earth itself can survive the fury of mounting dangers. We even speak of our age as post-Christian, as if the faith of Jesus is about to disappear among men. There is darkness still.

When Simeon prayed, "Lord, now lettest thou thy servant depart in peace . . . for mine eyes have seen thy salvation," it was not that he had a vision of a world about to emerge into utopia. It was simply that he now knew that the world had a Savior and that, come what may, he could be safe in his hands. Every follower of Jesus knows that. Each of us is an eternal creature. We are on the earth for a brief tenure. Death will overtake us, and one day (the day the Father himself decrees), the world itself will die, Christ will reappear in glory, and a new heaven and a new earth will unfold. Meanwhile, we rest in the everlasting arms, with our sins forgiven through this Jesus, and with our renewed rights to an eternal kingdom certain.

As we worship in our churches and hear the Word of promise again and again and lift our hearts in praise and thanksgiving, we too, with Simeon, can hold this Jesus and be held by him. We can walk out into the world of work and play with peace in our hearts and with minds captured by hope.

Song for Simeon

MELVA ROREM

Simeon was young; Simeon was young.
His dark eyes flashed with sure expectancy, sharing
the longings of his people, Israel, for the Messiah.
Did the young boy think of him, this infant
who would be "the everlasting Father,"
as he roamed the nearby hills of Judah-land?
As he crossed ravines with brooks—sometimes full
of water, sometimes only beds of stones?
As he heard the tinkling sounds of
camels on their way to market with their beads
and bells and laden humps? As he helped
his elders make grapes into wine, and milk into
cheese, and fleece into cloth? Deep in
his heart he knew that one day he would see
"the mighty God."

In the fulness of time, the Child was
born. One whirling star came to rest over a
stable in the hilltop town of Bethlehem.
Oxen, donkeys, turtledoves found rest in the shadows.
And Mary looked upon her newborn Child,
the Son of God, while angel choirs sang:
"A Child is born! Alleluia!"

Simeon was old; Simeon was old.
God's Spirit led him to the temple where he
mounted flight on flight of steps—
and there the mother, Mary, held her Son.
He took the Child into his arms with gentleness
and looked on him. A tiny hand rested
in his—like the spreading petals of a springtime
flower, he thought, or like another newborn star.
A swelling joy that was quiet and calm
and still filled his heart. And
he said: "Lord, now lettest thou thy servant
depart in peace . . . for I have seen. . . ."

Simeon was young; Simeon was young.
And he shared expectant longings of his people, Israel,
for the Messiah.
Simeon was old; Simeon was old.
And he held the promised one at last—
close to his heart.

A Penny for a Miracle

MELVA ROREM

RESEARCHED IN PART BY AGNES HARRIGAN MUELLER

A SMALL RAGGED newsboy stepped up to the stand in the lobby of a newspaper office in Philadelphia, laid down a penny and said, "Gimme one. M' sister's got it." The paper he carried that December morning in 1907 had shouted out the headline in large bold type, "Stamp out tuberculosis." Penny Christmas stamps were on sale for the first time in America to aid victims of this prevalent, dread disease. He dared to hope that a penny might help his sister.

The story begins earlier in Denmark. Einar Holboell, a postal clerk, was routinely sorting heavy Christmas mail when an idea flashed like a meteor into his mind. His thoughts were with children very dear to him who were suffering from tuberculosis. Suppose, it suddenly occurred to him, we could interest people in buying a special penny Christmas stamp to add to packages and letters during this season of goodwill and use the proceeds to help tubercular children. He dreamed on. . . . Suppose there might even be enough to start a hospital!

The Danish postmaster in Copenhagen liked Holboell's idea, and King Christian gave it his support. Danish citizens responded with enthusiasm, and in a short time the idea spread to neighboring Sweden, Norway, Iceland, and Finland. His idea had taken wings—an idea that in following years would circle the world.

A package that carried the Danish Christmas stamp was received in America by the famous and influential Danish-American writer, Jacob Riis. He was captivated by the penny stamp's possibilities as he thought of his six beloved brothers who had died of tuberculosis. His heart pounded with excitement and anticipation as he thought of what a great voluntary health organization could do to arrest the disease. He wrote a persuasive article for an American magazine, relentlessly pleading that the Christmas stamp idea be put in operation in America.

About the same time, Edward Livingston Trudeau, a young doctor in America, learned that he had TB. So feared was the disease at that time that it was called the white plague. It meant almost certain death, so Dr. Trudeau left the city to spend what he thought would be his few remaining years in his cottage at Lake Saranac in the Adirondack Mountains. But to his amazement, his condition improved. He felt better, stronger, and a measure of hope returned. He won-

Denmark, 1904

First Christmas seal

United States, 1907

First U.S. Christmas seal

"Sealscape"—United States, 1972

dered: *Is rest an important factor that helps the body heal itself of this disease?* Diligently, excitedly, he began to study the relationship between the symptoms of his illness and long periods of rest. Experimenting with this discovery, his simple mountain cottage was transformed into a two-patient hospital. And when it was obvious that rest helped others recover, money was raised for added buildings and necessary facilities.

The good news spread, and a group of doctors set up a small cottage-hospital on the banks of the Brandywine River in Delaware. Along with their friends and patients, they founded what is now known as the American Lung Association to promote the work. But, as happens so often in new ventures, lack of funds threatened the outcome; in 1907 a miracle was needed. And it happened. A big miracle! A lifesaving miracle!

Joseph Wales, one of the doctors of this group, asked for help from his cousin, Emily Bissell, who was an experienced fund raiser for the Red Cross in Wilmington, Delaware. The miracle began when she received Wales' letter almost simultaneously with reading the compelling article written by Jacob Riis. Could it be, she wondered, that the penny stamp idea might work here as well as in Denmark? Right here in Delaware? In neighboring states? From north to south in the United States, and from coast to coast?

Emily Bissell was a woman of action, and she decided to try. She designed the first stamp herself. With the cooperation of her Red Cross associates, she was allowed to use the Red Cross symbol. She added a wreath of holly and the traditional season's greeting, "Merry Christmas." With the help of her friends, 50,000 stamps and 2000 envelopes were printed, each envelope holding 25 stamps. A portion of the message on the envelope was: "Twenty-five Christmas stamps, one penny apiece, issued by the Delaware Red Cross to stamp out the white plague. These stamps do not carry any kind of mail, but any kind of mail will carry them."

The Christmas stamp was not a government issue, of course, so the post office could not promote it. But postal officials agreed to let Emily Bissell, the girl with a dream, set up a stand in their lobby where she could sell stamps. Sales were bleak—less than $25 a day. But Emily Bissell would not let the dream go. Instead, she helped make it come true. She went to Philadelphia to ask help from E. A. Van Valkenberg, editor of a leading newspaper, *The North American.* He was polite but totally uninterested in her idea. On her way out of the building she stopped to talk to Leigh Mitchell Hodges whose column, "The Optimist," she enjoyed. Years later, when Hodges had become known throughout the country as a dynamic speaker in the fight against TB, he wrote this account of his meeting that day with Emily Bissell:

> She opened the most capacious handbag I had ever seen, and out of it she took a sheet of those Christmas seals. I have no more understanding today than I did then, why at that moment I should have seen not small white squares of perforated paper, but a flaming banner—something to be carried at the head of hosts of all sorts of people to say to the world that the white plague could be prevented and cured.

United States, 1928

United States, 1931

United States, 1939

United States, 1942

United States, 1949

United States, 1952

United States, 1956

United States, 1962

United States, 1971

Hodges rushed downstairs two steps at a time and barged into the editor's office. Putting the stamps on the editor's desk, he shouted: "Here's what will stop TB. The way to fight this plague is to give the world the facts and teach them it can be prevented." The editor caught Hodges' contagious spirit, and Hodges went on: "How's this for a slogan? 'Stamp out tuberculosis!'" The editor offered the entire paper for the campaign. For three weeks Hodges wrote enthusiastically about the project, and the stamp appeared on every page. President Theodore Roosevelt and his cabinet, religious organizations, powerful social groups, the rich, the poor—all gave their support. More than 250,000 stamps were printed, and during the first year's appeal more than $3000 was raised. The hospital on the Brandywine was saved.

The American Lung Association united with the Red Cross to spread the word, to promote the sale of Christmas stamps (now called seals to distinguish them from postage stamps), and to give information concerning the rest treatment for TB. They issued a Christmas seal jointly in 1910, and the partnership continued until 1920, when the American Lung Association took over. The bright red double-barred cross, the Cross of Lorraine, appeared on the seal for the first time that year. Symbolizing hope and humanity, this cross was carried by Joan of Arc (born in Lorraine) when she raised the Siege of Orleans in 1429.

Eminent artists in the United States have contributed to the progress of Christmas seal campaigns by designing seals that convey the spirit of the endeavor. They shine with beauty, color, and simplicity, and always include the cheerful emblem of hope, the double-barred cross. Many less known and unknown artists have contributed attractive designs too. In 1975, 1977, 1978, and 1979, the art of 54 American children was used. Teachers asked children to make paintings that told what Christmas meant to them. The happy results revealed smiling snowmen, clear skies, mischievous elves, gift-laden Santas, friendly animals—all of them exuding the joy of the season. Writing about his own creation, Mark Lybrand of Lexington, South Carolina, said he had included Santa and his reindeer, snow, a sidewalk, a house, a Christmas tree, and a wreath. "Altogether," he went on, "my picture means that Christmas is a time of peace and goodwill." His postscript proved his personal goodwill: "You printed my Christmas seal backwards, but that's okay."

In 1976, Christmas seals had been designed and sold in 76 countries to fight TB and other lung diseases. There continues to be a delightful variety of stamps. Denmark (the originator of the idea) printed a likeness of their late Queen Louise on their first stamp. The Christmas story has been told through illustrations of Wise Men, the star, nativity scenes, and animals at the manger. Countries have issued sheets of seals where each seal forms part of a complete picture. In 1957, such a sheet of Danish stamps featured a parade of boats—from fishing skiffs, sailboats, and steamboats, to modern liners—each ship carrying a lighted evergreen. Similarly, in 1976, our bicentennial year, a "sealscape" design was created that represented scenes of rural America paralleling the 70-year history of the

United States, 1975

United States, 1975

United States, 1975

United States, 1975

United States, 1975

United States, 1975

American Lung Association. The designer was Bob Hungerford; the artist, Allan Mardon.

Stamps reveal both the historical and allegorical life of various countries. During turbulent years of German occupation, Norway's seals depicted peaceful scenes— a happy little boy, a small girl holding her Christmas doll in one hand and a candle in another, a Christmas bell painted above a winter scene, labeled *God Jul*. Finnish seals have lovely designs. One is a gleaming white snow scene with green trees against a blue sky, and a rabbit faces a squirrel as they look serenely at each other. Both France and Switzerland produce automobile windshield stickers which are enlarged replicas of their stamps. Belgium is one of the countries that makes poster-size seals for window displays. Seals may reflect the architectural designs of the countries that produce them, their geographical nature, their sports, flowers, and life-styles.

Modern medicines have made possible both the cure and prevention of TB today. Although the incidence of TB in our country has decreased greatly, there is a rise in other lung diseases. The same resources that fight TB are fighting these diseases. Over a million Americans have emphysema. Cases of chronic bronchitis and asthma bring the total to the colossal figure of 15 million persons who suffer today from lung diseases. Cost for medical care for these millions is colossal too. From 12 to 16 billion dollars are spent each year for medical care and personal expenses. Four hundred billion dollars are spent annually in social security disability payments.

The appalling figure of deaths from emphysema (the number of cases has doubled every five years since 1950) can be told. The number of cases of other lung-related diseases can be counted. Staggering sums spent for medicine and care can be quoted. These are measurable quantities. But who can measure the misery of those who suffer from these diseases? Who can know the dread in the hearts of those who hear the grim diagnosis and prognosis? Who can know the pain that permeates the lives of those afflicted and of those dear to them? For these are incalculable tragedies: they cannot be measured, and there is no scale on which they can be weighed.

Far horizons opened wide for Einar Holboell at the turn of the century in Denmark, and as a result, suffering from tuberculosis was eased for children. They opened wide for Americans who envisioned stamping out TB: Emily Bissell, Edward Livingston Trudeau, Jacob Riis, E. A. Van Valkenberg, Leigh Mitchell Hodges. They continue to open wide throughout our country annually as more than 60 million homes, businesses, and organizations include buying Christmas seals as part of their Christmas tradition.

"It has been said," Leigh Hodges wrote, "that I invented that newsboy. I'm not that clever. I couldn't have invented that combination of rags and skin-soil, nor the words he said. . . . But millions throughout the land have made the Christmas seal a most miraculous piece of paper. And the battle is not won until in all the land no one can say (of any preventable and curable lung disease), 'M' sister's got it.'"

Puerto Rico, 1957-1958

Australia, 1962

The Netherlands, 1966

Denmark, 1932

Guatemala, 1967

Iceland, 1930

Norway, 1929

India, 1946-1947

Victorian Toys

MARGARET REARDON

TO CELEBRATE the birth of a son and heir to the throne, Albert of Saxe-Coburg in Germany, Prince Consort of Queen Victoria, set up a small Christmas tree at Windsor Castle in 1841. "Today I have two children of my own to give presents to, who, they know not why, are full of happy wonder at the German Christmas tree and its radiant candles."

The Christmas Tree

The love of the English people for young Queen Victoria, their growing affection for Prince Albert, and their delight in the two children—the Princess Royal and their son, the new Prince of Wales—caused the loyal subjects to follow the example set by the royal family at Windsor. In every household the Christmas tree began to appear, trimmed with paper roses of gold foil, a few sweetmeats, and a number of penny toys. Small tapers twinkled on every branch. Actually, this was not the first Christmas tree in England. Many years before, Germans in the household of Queen Caroline had put up such a tree. In 1840, German merchants in Manchester, following the custom of their country, trimmed pine tops with 365 tapers—one for each day of the year. But it was the little tree at Windsor that established the custom of the Christmas tree in England.

The first tree at Windsor was itself a toy. From engravings in journals of that year, we see that it was a table tree, lighted with little tapers and hung with small toys—tin soldiers, drums, small lanterns, penny dolls, gilded nuts, bird cages, gingerbread men to be eaten when the tree came down, and the wax angel fastened on the topmost branch. Under the tree there were wooden soldiers, a jack-in-the-box, fleecy lambs, wooden trains, and the beloved Noah's ark.

Prince Albert, by setting up the tree at Windsor, was remembering Christmas Eve during his childhood, spent at Rosenau Castle in the Duchy of Saxe-Coburg. On that night the children of the household waited in breathless wonder outside the door of the "presents room" where the Christmas tree and a great number of gifts had been hidden for several days. When the last taper was lighted, the folding doors were flung back, and the children saw the tree, flickering with lights that revealed in its branches sugar plums and other delights so soon to be enjoyed.

The lovely thing about the Christmas tree of the last century was that its dismantling at Twelfth Night brought no sadness. The children were consoled by the feast provided by the candy and gingerbread toys.

Imagine biting into a sugar flute and finding it full of honey! In London, bakers specialized in making gingerbread toys at Christmas. These figures had come from the very old custom of eating bread dolls at fairs on feast days. The baker had many molds for these gingerbread toys made in the forms of animals, soldiers, and, of course, the gingerbread boy of storybook fame. The gingerbread toy was sprinkled with Dutch gilt and was sold at a reduced price when broken. That custom is the source of the saying, "the gold is off the gingerbread."

Wooden Toys

At that time, most toys were imported from Prince Albert's homeland, Germany, the great toy country of the world. His childhood home was close to the great forests of Thuringia where toymakers had long been famous. Snowbound in their forest homes and shut away from the world for months, whole families worked all winter carving wooden toys that were exhibited at fairs held in the spring.

The Noah's ark was made by one family in the

Dated at about 1830, these dolls are like those Victoria collected when she was a child. They are made of wood, jointed with wooden pegs. The woman doll is termed a "tuck comb" doll because of the comb tucked at the top of her head.

Thuringian forest for 50 years before it was made in England. Sometimes there were as many as 60 different animals in the ark, each carefully reproduced in wood. A family of toymakers might visit a zoological garden in a nearby city in spring or summer to study the anatomy of the animals they would carve during the long winter, or they might follow a circus. In England, the Noah's ark was known as a "Sunday toy"; it was the only toy with which a child could play on the Sabbath. It is believed that it was first made in Oberammergau.

Wooden toys predominated in the early days of Victoria's reign, and none was more beloved than the toy lambs made in Germany and sold on the streets of London. It is said that one family made 300 of these toys and covered them with wool from their own sheep. The toy lamb had a composition head of *papier maché,* with painted cheeks and eyes that were dabs of black paint. Their fleece was sprinkled with Dutch gilt, and they wore little red collars with bells. The toy peddler carried them through the streets of London in a basket strapped to his back, calling out one of the famous cries of London:

> Baa lambs to sell,
> baa lambs to sell.
> I have young pretty
> lambs to sell.

Wooden soldiers were also popular toys, often found under 19th century Christmas trees. They were also made from the great trees of the forests of Thuringia and were reproduced with great fidelity, dressed in scarlet jackets and bearskin caps.

This doll, a "covered wagon doll," has china arms, legs, and head. The doll's muslin body is stuffed with sawdust. Its dress is the style of 1840.

Model trains, now as popular with fathers as with sons, first were made in about 1840—a wooden locomotive and seven small coaches. This train was copied from the new Liverpool and Manchester Railroad that had been running only a few years. A model of "Stephenson's Rocket" had special appeal. Invented by George Stephenson, this locomotive was said to have terrific speed, and when the royal family rode in private coaches on their way to Balmoral, the queen had a signal installed that could warn the engineer to reduce the speed.

Another wooden toy of this period was the jumping jack, known in the Thuringian forest as a *Zappleman.* The jack-in-the-box sprang up when a lid was opened and a spring released—a great delight for Victorian children.

Small houses and churches arranged in a charming village scene under the old-time Christmas tree were made of wood and came from the Black Forest and from Austria. Alpine scenes from Switzerland or the Tyrol always featured a chalet set among tiny trees.

The rocking horse, another favorite, was at first simply a horse's head attached to a stick. They were called "hobby horses" and were used in the old morris dances—vigorous dances performed by men wearing costumes and bells. Later, the entire horse was carved out of solid wood and mounted on a platform with wheels. Then came the rocking horse, adorned with a mane, glass eyes, and a tail, and equipped with a bit and bridle.

"Pull toys" made of wood were mounted on platforms with wheels. When the small child pulled them with a string, a bell would ring, a wooden hen would peck, or a duck would quack.

Sound toys appealed to the young child in the 19th century as they do today. Often these toys were wound with a key. In his story, *The Nightingale,* Hans Christian Andersen features an artificial bird that can be made to sing by winding a key. These birds, operated with delicate mechanisms, were made of gold and were often jewel-studded. These, of course, were not playthings for children but were gifts for kings. When metal began to be used in making toys, there were many ingenious and amusing toys operated by winding a key. A soldier marched, measuring his own steps by beating a drum; a donkey pulled an old man in a cart.

For the sheer joy of making noise, boys of a century ago had plenty of whistles and horns on Christmas day. Sailor suits for boys at that time always came from the store with a whistle attached to a white cord so it could be placed in the top pocket.

The most charming of sound toys was the music box. Some of these had a small crank which, when wound, would play a tinkling little tune while a ballerina danced. When Victoria lived at Kensington Palace as a child, she had such a music box. She would lift the lid, and a stage would rise from the bottom of the box as three little figures danced until the tune stopped. Then the stage with the ballerinas descended to the bottom of the box.

This English hatted wax doll dates back to 1870-1875. Made of wax over papier maché, it has wooden arms and legs.

Dolls

Victoria's subjects often told the story of how, in 1837, two great couriers, the Archbishop of Canterbury and the Lord Chamberlain, had brought the news to young Princess Victoria at Kensington Palace that she had become the queen. These influential men had asked that the princess be awakened. When told by attendants that her Highness was asleep, the Archbishop of Canterbury had replied: "We have urgent business with Queen Victoria that must not be delayed." When Victoria left Kensington Palace as the Queen, she was 18 years old. Today, in that place where she was born, a record is preserved of her life as a child. In the palace is housed the London Museum, with her toys among its collections, the most famous being 132 of her dolls.

While a princess, Victoria chose to collect and dress the droll little wooden dolls. They measured from three to nine inches in height and were jointed at the arms and legs. Each doll represented some character prominent at that time—a lady at court, some famous actor or actress, a ballerina who was currently the rage in London. Victoria loved the ballet, so she dressed many of these little dolls as dancers. Mlle. Brocard was dressed in a white satin bodice with puffed sleeves and a silver tissue skirt. Marie Taglioni was Victoria's favorite ballerina, and she dressed this exquisite figure in a bodice of gold brocade and a bright red skirt for her role in *William Tell*. These doll clothes, sewed with fine stitching, were made during the years from 1831 to 1833. However, a piece of linen, yellowed with age, shows large stitches on a doll's dress made by Victoria at the age of four.

These wooden dolls, first made in Germany, were rather crude with carved faces. Unlike some of the wooden dolls with eyeballs inserted and wigs nailed on their heads, Victoria's little character dolls had painted features with hair represented by black paint. A copy book written by the little princess and still preserved, gives a list of the dolls. The name of each is given, the character it represents, and whether it was dressed by Victoria or by Baroness Lehzen, her governess. On the shoulder of each doll is a number that corresponds with the number on the list.

Dolls made history all through the reign of Victoria, from the time of the first wooden dolls to the great, beautiful wax dolls which won medals for Augusta Montanari, doll-maker at the Great Exhibition of 1851. This fair, held at the Crystal Palace in Hyde Park, was a dream that came true for Prince Albert. Among thousands of objects from far and near, none attracted more attention than the exhibition of toys.

Prominent among the doll-makers at that exhibition were members of the Montanari and the Pierotti families, long famous in England. Originally from Italy, Domenico Pierotti began to make dolls in London soon after his arrival there in 1780.

The wax doll became popular in England about 1820. Workers in wax are listed in old London directories. Artists had used wax models for centuries, and Madame Tussaud had come to London at the time of the French Revolution to open her famous waxworks.

During the early years of Queen Victoria's marriage, the wax doll became more and more popular. After the birth of her first two babies, toymakers in London designed wax dolls to look like the two young children. These were the first baby dolls. The Prince of Wales doll wears a dress like the doll representing the Princess Royal, Victoria Adelaide, but three royal plumes on his bonnet distinguish the heir to the throne. Both

These French fashion dolls are dressed in the styles of 1875. They have porcelain bisque hands and heads, kid bodies, and glass eyes.

dolls were made about 1845 and can be seen in the London Museum in Kensington Palace. Dolls of this type were called portrait dolls because they represented real persons, and frequently courtiers or other members of the royal family were depicted.

Nearly all wax dolls had blue eyes like the queen. Their faces, when marked by chubby fingers, could be washed with butter. While they were beautiful, they were too fragile for handling, and were sometimes put in glass-topped boxes in order to preserve them. This did not always please their young owners. A wax doll still exists which received so much affection that her nose is almost rubbed off with too many kisses!

About 1850, Augusta Montanari greatly beautified the wax doll by giving her real hair. By means of a hot needle, each hair was inserted into the wax scalp. This process was also used for eyebrows and eyelashes.

In order to make dolls for children more durable, a composition *papier maché* was used for the head, shoulders, and arms; this was then fitted on a body of kid filled with sawdust. Finally, a coating of wax over the compound gave beauty to the doll.

Bisque—porcelain without a glaze—was also used for dolls' heads, in the late Victorian period. Typically, these dolls featured lovely eyes and sweet expressions, endearing them to Victorian children. China and porcelain heads for dolls were easily imported because they were hollow and great numbers weighed so little.

One type of doll never designed to be cuddled or caressed was the fashion doll that originated in Paris and was often sent to foreign countries to display French fashions. Records indicate that, in 1396, Charles VI of France ordered a court tailor to send a doll with a complete wardrobe to his daughter, the child wife of Richard II. The popularity of the fashion doll declined when journals carrying news and pictures of prevailing modes appeared.

The "hobby horse" was a favorite with children of the Victorian period. This horse, carved from wood, is equipped with saddle and bridle.

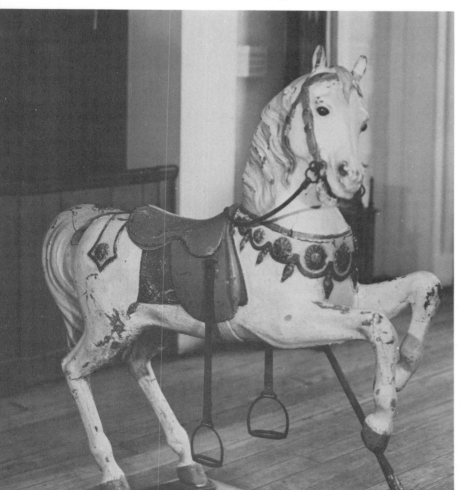

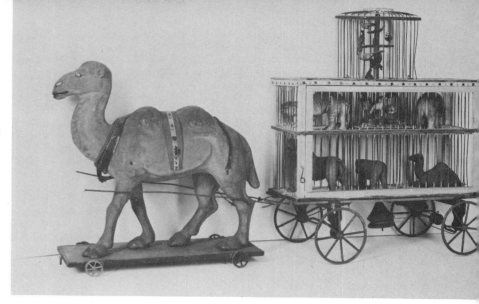

Pull toys were popular with English children. This wooden camel pulls a menagerie of smaller animals in the wagon behind him.

Toy Peddlers

The toyman of the streets of London was one of the most picturesque figures from a vanished past. He originated in medieval London and in the provinces where the wandering peddler set up his booth at a fair or, lacking a booth, spread out his wares on the street. At Smithfield Fair in 1133, toymakers sold dolls called "Bartholomew babies." The tribe of hawkers continued to flourish in London, pleasing children who had a mite to spend. When prices went up, children could still buy delightful "penny toys" sold on the streets—little sheep, a small pug dog, a miniature omnibus, or a pull-along horse that could go into a Christmas stocking. A friend of children, Ernest King, donated 1650 such items to the Children's Room in Kensington Palace.

Another character who walked the streets in Victorian times was the Peepshow Man. He carried a black box strapped to his back. A child could look into a magic world through a glass lens at the front of the box. Perhaps the child would see a lake, a little peasant figure on a road, and a castle in the background. Two or more tallow candles behind a screen gave the picture dimension. The crowds of children who followed this enchanting man could view a variety of scenes. *Queen Victoria's Coronation* was one of the most breathtaking scenes, never to be forgotten by the child who saw it. A verse taken from an old book was recited by the Peepshow Man who peddled magic for a penny:

> This box does pleasant sights enclose
> And landscape and perspective shows
> Of every varied sort.
> A penny is the price I ask
> For execution of my task
> And I get a penny for't.

Today toy peddlers have vanished from the streets of London. The little soldiers of that day are long since scattered. And the ballerina no longer dances to a lovely far-off tinkling tune. But Victorian toys remind us all of the special treasures of childhood that brought magic and mystery into our lives, special treasures that create a twinkling of excitement every Christmas.

25

Christmas Caper

R. D. STEVENS

"THEN YOU cannot help us, Monsieur De-meron?"

"Cannot!" the baker snorted, his eyebrows drawn fiercely together beneath the ever-present dusting of flour. "WILL not, you mean! Go ahead and say it, Brother Joseph; I know you think it! Help you and your good-for-nothing poor? I'd be taking the bread from my own mouth to feed those brats if you had your way! A priest-ridden village if I ever saw one!" His voice took on the cringing whine of a professional beggar. "Alms, for the love of God, alms. . . . A few sous, your worship? A cabbage leaf, madame, a crust of bread . . . ?"

Brother Joseph yanked the collar of his threadbare coat farther up around his ears and plunged from the warmth of the bakery out into the drizzle that was Proveleon. His thin, blue-veined hands trembled as he clutched at the crown of his hat, partly to keep the mistral from snatching it from his head, partly to hide the tears of vexation that stung his eyelids. No food for the poor, no food for the poor at Christmas, his

sandals seemed to repeat as they clattered over the cobbles, and the faces of Mario and Lepanto and Marguerite and all the others who'd held out their bowls for the last of the gruel that morning swam blurrily before him. And the donkey, thin sad beast that he was, had even stuck his head over the partition into the kitchen of the hovel and looked hopefully at him. Brother Joseph had given him the last remaining hay that morning—a few wisps and a corncob, and turned away quickly before the animal finished. There'd be no more tomorrow.

Brother Joseph stumbled as a gust of wind whipped the overly-large coat between his legs and he went down on his knees with a jar that wrung a cry of pain from him. There was a clink, and the few coins he'd been clutching in one hand rolled soullessly down the steep street toward the bay far below. Brother Joseph lurched to his feet, ignoring the pain in his knees. "The coins!" he cried. "For the poor!"

Half a dozen urchins darted from nearby doorways; eager hands snatched up the coins as they rattled past, and the street was empty once more.

"Michel!" Brother Joseph ordered. "Alain! I know you. Come back here with those coins!" Again he called, a note of desperation in his voice now, and finally a woman's arms thrust two reluctant little boys out into the street to face Brother Joseph. He looked the sullen little boys up and down, eyed the ribs visible through holes in their shirts, the bare feet blue with the cold, and sighed. "Keep them, young ones," he said as gently as possible, and sent them scooting back to their doorway. "You need them more than I."

Once again the street was empty.

Brother Joseph bent his head against the mistral and started for home. The hills of Proveleon were steep; the mistral strong; the sky a tattered gray that boded no good. He found himself wishing for his staff; the bruised knee

wouldn't bother him quite so much with a staff on which to lean. He stumbled onward, past the square of yellow light thrown by the tavern windows and paused for a moment by the door, set slightly ajar. The warmth, the fragrance of wine and roasting beef were almost too much for him; he turned giddy and would have fallen if it hadn't been for a hard-muscled arm that slipped around his shoulders and held him firmly until the dizziness passed and he could stand once more.

"Merci, M'sieur," he stammered, aware of the flush creeping up his cheekbones. "A momentary weakness; it is of no importance."

He felt the sudden sharp scrutiny of his rescuer and blushed the more for the figure he knew he must appear, an old man in threadbare clothing. Clean, it is true, and patched, but with a definite odor of donkey clinging to it. The stranger—for no villager wore a gray corduroy jacket and trousers, or expensive if well-worn boots—the stranger must think him a beggar. Even his robe had long since gone for a few more francs to help fill the mouths of his brood.

"In that case, M'sieur," the stranger's quiet voice murmured, "you could have no objection to joining us for dinner."

Brother Joseph's head came up, his weak eyes peered at his rescuer. "I—I have—just eaten," he muttered and turned his head away to hide the longing aroused in him by the sight of a sideboard set with roasts and breads of many kinds and cider, HOT cider.

The stranger glanced at his companion, until now half-hidden in the shadows, and raised one eyebrow inquiringly. The old man heard a merry laugh, felt a smooth cool arm slip around his waist, a tiny hand pat his old gnarled one. "Then of course you will join us for at least a mug of cider, Brother . . . ?"

Brother Joseph would not have been human if he hadn't reacted to the charm, the sympathy in that voice. "Joseph," he managed, and raised his head to gaze at one of the most enchanting young creatures

he'd ever met. Even the heavy seaman's sweater and beret could not hide the delicate triangle of a face, the huge dark eyes, the smoke and ivory that was Morgana, called "la fey." And of course Brother Joseph suffered himself to be led inside to a table and was seated across from the two young people, where the warmth of the fire could soak into his back, and somehow he found himself devouring a huge platter of roast beef while his host and hostess exchanged light banter. Brother and sister they were, on a cruise along the southern coast of France. Their sloop had been pinned in harbor by the mistral, and they didn't expect to sail until it abated. Actors, he thought he'd heard them say; at least they soon had him chuckling delightedly at their antics in one performance. It felt good to laugh again; it stretched long-unused muscles, and Brother Joseph found himself relaxing for the first time in months, basking in the warmth of the fire and the charm of his hosts.

"You are from Paris, then?" he asked, trying to place a faint *soupçon* that hinted of the North.

"Among many cities, M'sieur," the young man replied courteously and poured Brother Joseph another glass of cider.

"And you are actors?" Brother Joseph probed.

"Of a sort," the young man said and exchanged a secretly amused glance with his sister. "Of a sort."

Brother Joseph blushed. Perhaps it was the cider, or the warmth, but he was gabbling like an old gossip. "Forgive me," he said contritely. "I didn't mean to pry."

"You didn't." There was a hint of laughter in the young man's voice now, and Brother Joseph found himself studying him curiously. He was perhaps 28 or 29, with a thin, almost delicate face, dark eyes with a hint of jade to them, thin, well-cut lips. No one would ever call him handsome, but there was a certain lazy grace to his movements, a deftness with which he evaded Brother Joseph's questions that marked him as someone definitely—unusual.

It grew dark; the angelus was sounded, and Brother Joseph found to his dismay that he had talked for nearly two hours. Warm, relaxed, his stomach tight, and best of all, a kerchief full of beef slices to take home to his orphans, he found that he'd told his young hosts the whole story; it had spilled from him like poison spilling from a half-healed wound.

Proveleon was not a wealthy village, to be sure; the fishing had gone since the harbor silted up, and the thin, rocky soil did not produce much. But the people, God willing, were able to put a little something into the poor box now and then: a few sous, a few wizened apples, ducks' eggs, a cabbage or two. And the children helped. They were all orphans, many of Spanish or Algerian descent and, therefore, outcast. But the boys fished and hunted shellfish in the tide pools, while the girls hired out to clean and took turns herding the donkey up to the cliff pastures. Everyone shared alike, down to the last mussel divided between all 12, or the last apple shared with the donkey. But the offerings grew fewer and the odd jobs harder to find, until at last the orphans were actually starving— the boys so weak their muscles trembled in spasms from the least exertion. Brother Joseph had watched with despair, spent every franc of his savings and his meager war veteran's pension on them, but still the day came when nothing was left. He'd gone out that morning, determined to find help, only to be told with the inevitable shake of the head that the saints must provide, mortal man had done all he could. Nowhere was he offered a scrap of work, a crust of bread, a suet pudding—although the smells of the butcher's shop had made his mouth water. And surely those were

new shoes the greengrocer's wife was wearing? And wasn't the shoemaker's family looking fat and fit, and the grain in the miller's warehouse almost overflowing? But the baker was the worst. A devout atheist, he proclaimed himself, though when he'd had the pox he'd been quick enough to yell for the priest. A child hater too. Orphan he'd been, he bragged at the tavern; man and boy, he'd risen by the seat of his own brow, and everyone else could too. The holy Sisters of Mercy, who'd secured him an apprenticeship as a baker, were conveniently forgotten. No sniveling was going to get so much as a petit pan from him. And when Brother Joseph, shivering with the cold, had pleaded with him, he'd been driven with curses out into the streets.

When the old man had gone, with many thanks and a lightness to his step that had been absent many a day, the two young people sat quietly, lost in thought. Remembering, perhaps, other orphans and times not so long past.

"Act One," said the young man thoughtfully, "to the baker." And he frowned into his wineglass.

"Act Two," nodded Morgana. "The plot thickens."

"Act Three." The young man glanced up, smiling at Morgana's eagerness. "About to begin."

The mistral blew itself out two days later, but still the sloop belonging to the two young strangers tugged at her moorings in the harbor. They'd found the village pleasant, they replied courteously when asked, and the seafood good. Often they strolled the cobbled streets, pausing now and then to peer inquisitively into shop windows—the bakery, for example, where M. Demeron and his wife made those luscious rolls and breads and cakes that were displayed in the window. If they settled themselves on benches on the shady side of the inn and if their glances often strayed to the bakery directly across from them until they knew the ritual of M. Demeron's day as well as he, why, it was cool there, and shady, and the scent of roses pleasant.

The tiled roofs of Proveleon were already pink with the dawn when M. Ambroise, the policeman, turned into the main street. He had walked his small beat for 20 years without discovering more than a strayed goat in someone's garden. And he therefore amused himself by making his stride as regular, as mechanical as that of the sergeant of the gendarmerie, whose keppie, if nothing else, he admired. So it was this morning. Two strides, flash his light at the door of the butcher's shop, rattle the handle; another few strides, the grocer's shop.

M. Ambroise then did something he had never done before. He actually broke that well-practiced stride and came to an astonished halt. Village gossips would shake their heads over so momentous an event for years afterward. But quickly M. Ambroise's nose confirmed what his eyes had told him. M. Demeron the baker never, but never came to work before nine. At precisely that hour he would stalk down the street, produce a large key, and open the bakery. He had never varied the ritual in the 20 years M. Ambroise had been village policeman. Yet today, Christmas morning,

the baker's shop was open, the red light of dawn reflected in its windows. M. Demeron himself in his
white apron was sweeping off the steps, and his wife,
that silent, long-suffering woman, was in the back of
the shop taking bread from the ovens with the paddle.

"Good morning, M. Demeron," M. Ambroise called,
not expecting an answer, and turned away, back to his
beat. But then the second surprise of that memorable
morning occurred. M. Demeron dropped his broom
and ran toward the policeman, overwhelming him with
a hug. "M. Ambroise, the very man! Come, try a croissant; they are fresh from the oven. And a roll, or a
petit pan—perhaps you would prefer some cake!"

M. Ambroise found his arms filled with the fragrant
morsels and could only stare, bewildered, at M. Demeron. "Are you feeling all right, M. Demeron?" he
inquired solicitously. "Your liver has perhaps been
troubling you?"

The baker laughed and clapped him on the shoulder.
"The old woman and I are playing Pere Noël today,
M. Ambroise, that is all. I am selling all my pastries at
half price this morning, the breads at two for a franc.
Or even—" he shot a sly glance at his wife and lowered
his voice "—five napoleons for a KISS! No, don't look
at me like that, man, I'm not crazy! My wife and I,
we planned this—a Christmas surprise for the whole
village. Go on now, M. Ambroise, try them, they are
very good," and he went back to his ovens.

Before M. Ambroise could begin on his eclairs, the
fragrant smell of hot rolls had drifted out into the
streets, and a stray child appeared, and then another.
It was not unknown for these street urchins to distract
a merchant long enough for another to snatch an apple
or perhaps a loaf of bread or even a sausage, and dash
off with it, handing it off to another if the angry pur-
suer got too close. But no sooner had they appeared
this morning than M. Demeron himself appeared on
the steps of the bakery, not waving his bread paddle

at them as usual, but with his apron overflowing with
rolls. Such a swarm of hungry, half-clothed little starve-
lings was never seen before or since! And by the
time the sun was fairly up, the street was thronged
with cheerful crowds, maidens laughing as they exchanged a kiss for five napoleons or a peck on the
cheek for a croissant. Soon the baker's counters were
bare, his money box heaped with francs, sous, a few
lire, the beggars staggering homeward under great
loads of bread. Brother Joseph and his crew of hungry
orphans were munching on rolls; even the donkey had
his few. Quiet came back to the street. One by one,
the lights in the baker's shop were turned off, cupboard
doors hastily shut, the coins scooped up into a canvas

bag, and M. Demeron and his wife slipped wraith-like
into the shadows that still lingered in the streets.

M. Demeron, the baker, took his great key from his
pocket and unlocked the door of his shop. It was nine
o'clock Christmas morning, and the slanting rays of
the early sun were beginning to reach his windows. He
padded across the floor, ignoring the light switch. Why
waste electricity, was his philosophy, when in a little
while the sun would provide light, and he knew his
way blindfolded? A thrifty man, the baker. He felt the
familiar roughness of his apron on the peg where it

always hung, tied it around him, then turned sleepily to the flour bins. He pulled one open, reached inside. His fingers encountered only hard wood. He groped further, still half asleep, and found nothing. With a grunt he turned and padded across to the fireplace. A little light would soon put things to rights; he must have reached into the wrong cupboard.

The flames licked hungrily around the log he tossed in, sending shadows flickering across the ceiling. Surely that would dispel this nightmare born of sour wine and greasy bacon! He thrust his head into the bin and stared in disbelief. Empty! He patted the wood mechanically, but found only a trickle of flour in the far corner. With a queer feeling in his stomach, he crossed to the other cupboards and yanked them open. They, too, were empty.

He switched on the lights, ignoring the fact that the sun would soon be pouring its beams into the shop, and stood aghast. The shelves were all empty; the oven still glowing. There were fingerprints on his glass counter, trails of flour from the cupboards to the mixing tables.

The roar that followed brought M. Ambroise running from the tavern where he was relaxing over a late breakfast. A deliriously happy Brother Joseph, the mayor, and many of the townspeople followed.

"M. Demeron!" they shouted, surrounding him with sticky fingers and jelly-ringed mouths and enthusiastic embraces. "We love you!"

"Police!" M. Demeron managed to yell, freeing himself with difficulty from the grasp of two of Brother Joseph's orphans. That worthy stepped forward, his face beaming, "It was a wonderful thing you did, M. Demeron, the best Christmas the town has ever had. And to think that, if it hadn't been for the two young strangers who saw you sneak up to the orphanage and leave the money, we would never have guessed!" A

babble of sound, of congratulations drowned out the baker's incoherent replies, until he stood helplessly silent, his face turning beet red.

"Such a large amount of money, too!" put in one of the wives. "It should feed the orphans for many months. Even, perhaps, some schooling. . . ."

M. Demeron's face drained quickly of color, became its normal pasty white. Quite suddenly exhausted, he groped for a chair.

"But . . . but . . . I didn't . . ." he stammered.

"No false modesty is permitted, M. Demeron!" the mayor said, patting his shoulder kindly. "You shall have a medal at the least! A statue, if the funds can be found!"

"How did you do it?" chorused all the voices, and M. Demeron saw around him all the people of the village he'd known—and yet not known—for so many years. There was Mme. Reboult, her gouty leg not so funny any more, her face beaming with tears of joy; and the postman, retired for years, waving one of the baker's best soft rolls. M. Demeron felt his miser's heart contract at the sight. And the urchins nestled trustingly around his knees, getting sticky fingers on his expensively-polished shoes.

Somewhere inside him a hard, ugly scab broke loose.

He took a deep breath and tried hard to look sly. "It wasn't easy," he began. "We had to fool you all, my old woman and I. . . ."

"Ahhh?" they breathed.

M. Demeron settled down to talk, his gestures growing more expansive, his voice more confident as his tale unfolded. He laid a floury finger aside his nose. "It was this way, you see. . . ."

At the back of the crowd stood the two young strangers, almost invisible in the shadows of the greengrocer's shop. M. Ambroise might, if he hadn't been listening so avidly to M. Demeron's tale, have noticed a trace of makeup beneath the young man's jaw, the smudge of flour on his sister's elbow. But M. Ambroise had just finished his patrol, his stomach was tight with croissants and orange jelly and onion soup, and the warm sunlight was beating into his shoulders and gradually turning his bald spot pink.

The young man winked at his sister, and together they turned to leave.

Pictured here in about 1955, Randolph Haugan and Lee Mero survey some of the artwork Mr. Mero had prepared for Christmas.

Lee Mero

MELVA ROREM

IT IS SOMETHING of an impossibility to write about the artist, Lee Mero, without writing too about Randolph Haugan, editor of *Christmas* the past 50 years. For during the years that Mero contributed an eight-page picture-story reminiscing about Christmas during "the good old days," the pages were signed, "the editor and the artist." On these pages they worked together; they complemented each other as few people do who combine ideas that emerge as art and words. And they had such a good time doing it that anyone walking by Haugan's office when the door was open (a hard-to-find, unidentified back office at Augsburg Publishing House, just off a stockroom, that Haugan occupied regularly as general manager and irregularly after retirement as he continued to edit *Christmas*) would vicariously enjoy their contagious chuckles and expressions of enjoyment, and wonder what they were up to in this particular section. Aside from the skills involved, that the work was done with such wholehearted joy could be one of the chief reasons for its widespread appeal and success.

"This was the routine," Haugan explained recently. "Lee would come to my office, and we'd discuss what his next section might be about. He'd say what he'd like to do, and I'd offer any suggestions I had." Haugan paused, remembering, and smiled as he added, "He'd use about two percent of my suggestions."

"He'd come back with sketches that only he could understand," Haugan continued, "but the ideas were always good, and I knew it was going to be just what we wanted. When he brought in the finished art, it always was, and we'd add the names we wanted for stores, towns, and people. His marvelous humor permeated every page. I recall that on one page he included a sketch of a favorite aunt wearing a fur coat. And Mero happily commented, 'I always wanted to give my aunt a fur coat!'"

On the pages where his picture-stories appear, Mero wandered through yesterday's world with reality and accuracy. Men, women, and children appear and speak to us of yesterday, even as they are caught up in their own exciting Christmas world which we are privileged to enter as guests. His figures are small, but they are infused with so much energy and old-fashioned splendor, that they seem life-size. Nothing great or small in that world is foreign to him. He pushes back the shadows and brings to light with painstaking accuracy the ordinary, everyday elements of yesterday's Christmas that brought joy to everyone—grandparents, parents, aunts, uncles, young folks, children, and family friends.

For old-time Christmases and other articles, maps, and books that called for historical facts (and he was a stickler for accuracy) he had a fascinating collection of reference books. Among them were a variety of

31

catalogs, including the Sears Roebuck catalog as far back as 1901, a tremendous collection of *National Geographic* and countless other magazines. He liked having a studio in his home where he could be his own boss, but that didn't keep him from working "a regular shift." He had specified hours and worked a five-day week. "It's the only way you can get anything done," he often said. Readers from all parts of the country who enjoyed his picture-stories sent him pictures, stories, and incidents from their own past too. A message would come on a postcard: "Say, do you remember the way we used to string popcorn and cranberries for the tree? Six pops to one cranberry. . . ." And if it was something he incorporated into the next year's story, the reader who sent the card might find his own name slyly inserted at that point.

RANDOLPH HAUGAN has said: "You put a man in a particular place—the right place. You leave him alone, and soon he has carved out a little kingdom. Nobody can convince him that his isn't the most important job in the place." Although Lee Mero did free-lance work for Haugan, he must have felt this spirit in his work on *Christmas*. Surely he carved out his little kingdom as he worked on *Christmas*, enjoying Haugan's rare combination of freedom and restraint as they worked together.

Lee Mero was born in Ortonville, Minnesota, "a long time ago," as he put it. He lived in Wisconsin for a few years and moved to Minneapolis with his family when he was four. But he had learned to love small towns and the countryside, and as a boy he went back to Wisconsin to spend time with his aunts and uncles. He loved the woods, streams with trickling waters, bird songs, autumn's woodsmoke, and the quiet snowy days and nights of winter.

His studies in art began at the Minneapolis School of Art with Robert Koehler when it was still a part of the old city library at Tenth Street and Hennepin Avenue. Later he studied at the Chase Art School in New York under Robert Henri. While there he shared a combination studio and apartment with two Minneapolis friends. Unaware that World War I had been declared, these young artists were sketching down at the waterfront. They were arrested as spies, and the three naive men were taken to court, declared to be off United States limits. Fortunately, their explanation was feasible.

When Mero came back to Minneapolis, he worked for the Federal Schools (now the Bureau of Engraving), and for the MacMartin advertising agency. In 1920, he and Kathryn Rice of Fargo, North Dakota, were married. At this time he was working in Chicago for the Charles Daniel Frey Advertising Agency, and among other things, he did Coca Cola ads in which he began doing the type of line drawings of small town goings-on with which readers of *Christmas* are so familiar.

Returning to Minneapolis, he became head of the art department at the George Buzza Company where

Christmas cards were created and produced. He began free-lance work in 1937, doing a number of assignments for Ernest Dudley Chase in Boston. It was during this period that a Minneapolis poet, Larry Hawthorne, introduced Mero to editor Haugan. A wonderful working relationship began that continued until Mero's death in 1977.

"In all those years," Haugan commented, "there wasn't one unpleasant experience."

Lee Mero's art contains a rich and diverse selection of illustrations, calligraphy, book jackets, and maps. Among the books he illustrated for Augsburg Publishing House (sometimes writing the copy too) were: *Muskego Boy* by Edna Hong, several books by Grace Noll Crowell, *My Christmas Book, Little Rhymes from A to Z,* and *Christmas Promise.* He did a perceptive and illuminating series of maps that detailed the work and travels of the apostle Paul. His first contribution to *Christmas* was the illustrations for the Christmas Gospel in 1937. Other work for the Christmas annual includes art for seven covers, artwork in a number of issues for the Christmas Gospel, illustrations for stories, articles, and poetry, and the eight-page picture-stories where his art celebrated yesterday's Christmases and became a regular feature.

Children wrote letters to the publishing house and to Lee Mero telling him how his work delighted them. Older people, who had lost sight of their growing-up years, wrote that nostalgically he had recaptured those years for them with his drawings. His work spoke to hundreds of readers, stirring memories of yesteryears. With his restless imagination and in his unpretentious way, Mero offered himself to the people in his unique everyday art.

I was privileged to be present during one of the last conversations Randolph Haugan had with Lee Mero. Kathryn, Mero's beloved wife, was there too, and at one point she said: "We've lived too long, but we're not going to die. Life is so exciting!" Mero was weak and frail, but the same bright light flashed in his eyes. The wit, the keen perception, the friendly warmth—all were there. I thought of a story I had heard about John Quincy Adams when he was in his 80s, and paraphrasing a bit to fit our artist friend, it would go like this:

> A friend stopped by and asked, "And how is Lee Mero today?" To which he replied: "Lee Mero is very well, thank you. But the tenement he's been living in all these years is beginning to show the ravages of time. With every wind it groans as if to crumble. One of these days Lee Mero will need to find new quarters. But Lee Mero himself is very well."

Artist Robert Henri, one of Lee Mero's much-loved teachers, has said: "All great works of art look as if they were done in joy." Mero must have taken that great truth and held it in his heart. For not only his art but his life was also a constant manifestation of joy.

MEMORIES are a part of CHRISTMAS

A Picture Story by LEE MERO

Aunt Mary's Coffee Mill

Mary's red tricycle

first Stocking Cap

buck-wheat cakes

blackstrap

Norm Groth's home-made sleigh

jingle jingle

Once again it is the Season of Remembrance!

For those readers who would care to forget this HI-FI, fast-traveling jet age we are living in ——for about ten minutes —— let's go back down (as it has been called poetically) "Memory Lane" to the days of a somewhat quieter era.

The Editor and the Artist

read on ➤

"Keeping up with the Social Procession" is an old American custom and in the cities, Afternoon Teas were popular during the holidays around 1900.

The casual caller always presented a card to the maid

To pep up little ol' last Fall's gown, Ladies' Home Journal presented "Three Stylish Fronts".

And no front hall was worthy of the name unless it had a card tray

According to a mail order catalog one could smell like Hyacinth, Violet, Tube Rose, Crab Apple, Shannon Bells, Wild Rose, Sweet Clover, New Mown Hay (that's what it said) for from 20 to 30 cents an ounce.

Remember?

and, once past the maid and the front hall, you might have seen a living room like this!

"TIMES-AREN'T-WHAT-THEY-USED-TO-BE" item

COMIN

Agnes and Mildred

NOW and THEN

Cast an eye on this etiquette note of 1904

In a girl's first season her mother usually gives the invitation to young men to call upon her, but later a girl may do so on her own behalf. Such invitation should not be given at a first meeting, unless some mutual friend has planned to bring them together, or the man is a relative of an intimate friend.

haven't you heard

Sue Platou   Carolyn Schroder

NO!   Evelyn Helgeson

delighted   Mari   Bede   Kathryn   charmed
"I'm sure."

Louise   Clara   Ingeborg   lovely afternoon   Agnes
and SHE said   Martha   Iva   Evelyn Stenson   and I said

They left their cards

a **C**hic Shopper   our Mary

Ah, for the good ol' days when maids were maids (and about a dime a dozen)

Somewhere among 'em, we'll wager there was a gran'ma who "just happened to have a picture of her latest grandchild" with her.

"She's a darling"   "Just like her mother"

a Zouave! how CUTE!   "Isn't that sweet?"

Terry PHOTOGRAPHER   Joan Photographer   S. Ingvaldson Studios   ELLS Photo Gallery

Children's parties haven't changed much—But their clothes have!

oh dear oh dear

Niagara Falls!   Kathy   MA-MA-A-A!   Mark

Jeff   Lynn   Randy   it's mine!   it's MINE

Lucinda   Kelly   Paul   Gib   Jon

(did we say, "a somewhat quieter era" on page 1?)

Back in the days before "ranch-house ramblers," houses came BIG— and mother, father, several children as well as gran'ma and gran'pa frequently all lived together under one roof (and maybe sometimes a shirt-tail relative or two)

Aunt Kathy's attic bedroom

She always slept with her head pointing North. In that way, the polar current struck vertically through her body toward her feet! In 1897 she read where some scientists said so! (The result? we haven't found out)

It made quite a gathering when "company" came for Christmas

Mister Hans Schwarz the grocer and Mister Arnie Peterson the milkman were steady callers and it took a lot of "cutting up" on the part of Mister George Nordwall the butcher; to keep supply meeting demand.

ANNUAL JOKE
Uncle Charles always waited till the women-folks were dog-tired from shopping, clean-ing, baking, cooking, etc, before quipping "Yup, you're just the WEAK before Christmas!"

CHRISTMAS DINNER
(Please;— just picture for yourself what a lot of folks eating a lot of food should look like.

While dinner was going on downstairs, the children were herded upstairs to wait for second table.

The spare chamber, with its closets, chests and chimney corner, afforded plenty of space for "Hide-and-seek", and "Puss-wants-a-corner".

8-9-10— here I come!

And mischievous youngsters loved to dress up with hats and wraps left lying on the spare bed by the visitors.

Ruth Peterson thought Mrs. Walt Schmidt's "Creation" was very becoming!

I'm too warm

J.M. Wickman looked like a "swell" with Mr. Christenson's Derby and cane

Mrs. Carl Platou long black gloves were too long on one end to fit

There was a lot of pre-holiday activity at the crossroads church with its bazaar, choir rehearsals and tableaus.

HOME MADE

NO-WEL-L-L

That's for us!

The street lamps on the corners were all shined up.

Mrs. Ingbritsen's Sunday school class spruced up the spruce in the church yard with tidbits for the birds.

Florence

Careful, Miss Daniels, not so many peanuts!

Ducey

Ann

Willing workers filled candy bags and strung popcorn and cranberries.

KLUNK

CLATTER BANG

Gifts ranged from a watch and chain $14.60

Supt Sidney Rand of the Sunday School received a "cut glass" sugar and cream set $1.85

for the Pastor to a hand bag for the woman who "came in" to do the dishes after church suppers

$1.37

When wasn't a Christmas sermon punctuated by a caretaker taking care of a furnace?

Pastor Alvin Rogness' wife cheered homes of "shut-ins" with little boxes of Nora's home-made divinity fudge.

Children learned the joy of giving when they brought toys for the "Christmas Sled" and took them to children on the "other side of the tracks."

Connie and Art

(a requested reprint)

Go Tell It on the Mountain

Negro spiritual, refrain
John W. Work Jr., 1871 - 1925, stanzas, alt.

Negro spiritual

Refrain

Go tell it on the moun - tain, O - ver the hills and ev - 'ry where;

Go tell it on the moun - tain That Je - sus Christ is born!

1. While shep-herds kept their watch-ing O'er si - lent flocks by night, Be-
2. The shep-herds feared and trem-bled When, lo, a - bove the earth Rang
3. Down in a lone - ly man - ger The hum - ble Christ was born; And

Refrain

hold, through-out the heav-ens There shown a ho - ly light.___
out the an - gel cho - rus That hailed our Sav - ior's birth.___
God sent us sal - va - tion That bless - ed Christ-mas morn.___

Away in a Manger

American, 1885   American, 19th cent.

1. A - way in a man-ger, no crib for his bed, The little Lord Je-sus laid down his sweet head; The stars in the sky . . . looked down where he lay, The little Lord Je-sus a-sleep on the hay.

2. The cat-tle are low-ing; the poor ba-by wakes, But little Lord Je-sus no cry-ing he makes. I love you, Lord Je-sus; look down from the sky And stay by my cra-dle till morn-ing is nigh.

3. Be near me, Lord Je-sus; I ask you to stay Close by me for-ev-er and love me, I pray. Bless all the dear chil-dren in your ten-der care And fit us for heav-en to live with you there.

O Little Town of Bethlehem

Phillips Brooks, 1835-1893

Lewis H. Redner, 1831-1908

1. O lit-tle town of Beth-le-hem, How still we see thee lie!
2. For Christ is born of Mar - y, And, gath-ered all a - bove
3. How si-lent-ly, how si-lent-ly The won-drous gift is giv'n!
4. O ho-ly Child of Beth-le-hem, De-scend to us, we pray;

A - bove thy deep and dream-less sleep The si - lent stars go by;
While mor-tals sleep, the an - gels keep Their watch of won-d'ring love.
So God im-parts to hu - man hearts The bless-ings of his heav'n.
Cast out our sin, and en - ter in, Be born in us to - day.

Yet in thy dark streets shin - eth The ev - er-last-ing light.
O morn-ing stars, to - geth - er Pro-claim the ho - ly birth,
No ear may hear his com - ing; But, in this world of sin,
We hear the Christ-mas an - gels The great glad tid-ings tell;

The hopes and fears of all the years Are met in thee to - night.
And prais-es sing to God the King, And peace to all the earth!
Where meek souls will re-ceive him, still The dear Christ en - ters in.
Oh, come to us, a - bide with us, Our Lord Im - man-u - el!

'Twas in the Moon of Wintertime

Jean de Brebeuf, 1593 - 1649
tr. Jesse E. Middleton, 1872 - 1960, alt.

French folk tune, c. 16th cent.
arr. Austin C. Lovelace

1. 'Twas in the moon of win-ter-time When all the birds had fled,
2. The ear-liest moon of win-ter-time Is not so round and fair
3. O chil-dren of the for-est free, The an-gels' song is true.

That God, the Lord of all the earth, Sent an-gel choirs in-stead.
As was the ring of glo ~ ry A-round the in-fant there.
The ho-ly child of earth and heav'n Is born to-day for you.

Be-fore their light the stars grew dim, And won-d'ring hunt-ers heard the hymn:
And when the shep-herds then drew near The an-gel voic-es rang out clear:
Come, kneel be-fore the ra-diant boy, Who brings you beau-ty, peace, and joy.

Je-sus your king is born! Je-sus is born! Glo-ry be to God on high!

Sing Alleluia

Melva Rorem

Paul Fetler

Lively, with expression

mp
mp
mf

1. The stars hung low o-ver Beth - le - hem,
2. The Wise Men saw... one shin - ing star,
3. They gave their pre-cious gifts   to him,

Oh,_____   oh,_____ When Mar- y's child...was born ....   Oh,_____
Oh,_____   oh,_____ That shat-tered dark with a shaft of light.   Oh,_____
Oh,_____   oh,_____ They bowed and knelt...a - part ....   Oh,_____

Americana

TEXT BY MELVA ROREM

ILLUSTRATIONS BY WILLIAM MEDCALF

THE TRUE spirit of Christmas is always anchored in the centuries-old Christmas story. It was so in the latter part of the 19th century in America and in the early 20th century, just as it is in Christian homes today. Father, then as now, gathered the family about him and read the treasured biblical account of Jesus' birth. Its mystery and wonder could never be exhausted as he led them in thought from the home of Mary and Joseph in the hills of Nazareth, on and on long, weary miles to the gates of Bethlehem, and at last to the manger where Mary's child was born. On the following pages, special occasions that were the essence of these earlier Christmas days are captured in illustration and word—memories from Illinois, Wisconsin, North Dakota, Kansas, Arizona, and Iowa.

Thanksgiving had been a day of praise and gratitude. Christmas was a day of joy. There was the ringing joy of bells: the tiny tinkle of individual sleigh bells; the bobsleds' long, silvery bell strands that hung over harnesses; and church bells ringing out the message, "Christ has come!" There was the quiet joy of lamplight and candlelight. There was the heady joy of tantalizing aromas coming from the kitchen. Gifts were lovingly made and lovingly given, with joy: hand-knit socks and ties and mittens; crocheted yokes for nightgowns; tatted collars for blouses; cornhusk dolls with prune faces and dresses made from scraps of cloth and bits of ribbon; whittled toys that were treasured whether they were made with skill or lack of it. And always there was the festive joy of song: tender lullabies; boisterous medleys; stirring choruses; carols from other homelands; and American carols such as "We three kings of Orient are" (1857), "I heard the bells on Christmas Day" (1863), "It came upon the midnight clear" (1900); "O little town of Bethlehem" (1893).

Many of the elders, remembering their native homes with an almost aching longing, returned in spirit to far-off lands where they had known Christmas in their growing-up years. And remembering, they brought to their new homes customs from their homelands that we still enjoy today.

The Germans and Swiss skillfully carved wooden figures for the family Christmas crèche. Families from Denmark held hands and circled the Christmas tree, singing their carols. In the center of their little villages in Pennsylvania, the Moravians erected the *putz*, and live animals gathered round the manger. Norwegians tied large sheaves of grain to the top of a pole and fastened choice bits of suet here and there for the birds. A custom from Sweden celebrated St. Lucia's Day on December 13th, when the oldest daughter, often chosen as the family's St. Lucia, served coffee and Lucia buns to members of the household as they awakened.

Dutch settlers celebrated the coming of St. Nicholas on December 6 when, wearing his embroidered robe, his miter, and his crozier, he placed gifts in the shoes of the children. The Irish brought the custom of placing a lighted candle in each window on Christmas Eve to burn through the twelve nights of Christmas. Caroling on city streets and country roads was a tradition brought from "merrie England." Such caroling could be heard in the courtyard of Baltimore's Old Colony Inn in our country too, and in various other localities, much like it was at English inns as guests arrived for Christmas in sleighs and bobsleds. In Connecticut sleighs seemed to fly up hill and down with singing carolers.

An ancient legacy of Spain was the traditional lighting of little fires and *luminarias*. The custom was revived in the old Southwest, New Mexico and southwestern Texas, when in early days the nights were brightened with small bonfires called *farolitos* made of fragrant piñon boughs brought down from the mountains. Later, lights of candles in paper bags, called *luminarias*, burned along driveways, walks, and flat roofs of homes. Italians brought with them the custom of having a *presepio*, or crib, in every home, even the poorest. The family made this a replica of Christ's birthplace, the holy family, Wise Men, shepherds, and an empty manger which awaited the Christ child's coming on Christmas Eve when a baby doll was placed there.

Christmas is always a returning home, even if it is only a returning of the heart and mind. In earlier days, members of families often lived closer together, and going home for Christmas in a bobsled or by other horse-drawn vehicles was possible. The rushing whir of shining steel runners sliding over snow and ice, or the steady beat of the horses' hoofs, seemed to echo the simple cry in the hearts of all: "Home! Home! Home for Christmas!"

Christmas in America was not like Christmas in any other land. It was like Christmas in many lands. For people from other countries brought to their new homes rich treasures of custom and tradition. Into the pattern that became America's Christmas, colorful threads of Christmas from everywhere were woven. And each thread became part of the varied, nostalgic tapestry that was Christmas in early America.

Kansas

At the turn of the century, the stagecoach, a horse-drawn passenger coach that also carried mail, brought relatives and friends together at Christmas time. These Kansas families remembered when they celebrated Christmas in their "soddies," snug against the winds of winter. Now, they were building more modern homes.

Germans from Russia, fugitives from the czarist rule, joined them, bringing their Christmas customs with them. One custom involved a Christmas herald. A lady, dressed in white with a wide blue sash, would come to every home as the herald of *"Christ Kindlein"* (Christ child). The waiting family would hear the tinkle of a little bell, and she would enter with the greeting *"Gelobt sei Jesus Christus"* ("Praised be Jesus Christ"). After the youngest child said a Christmas prayer, the herald would throw gifts—a quantity of nuts—into the air. And as the children scrambled about to get them, she would disappear.

Swedish folks in early Kansas demonstrated the best example of Scandinavian customs. Christmas Eve celebrations were family affairs, unless a nearby stranger who was alone was invited in. The finest supper possible was served, "a feast of the hearts," and gifts were opened beside the tree. As early as five o'clock the next morning, everyone gathered at the church for *Julotta,* the special Christmas service. Sleighs carried each family along as songs and greetings of *"God Jul"* rang through the cold, crisp air. Father stood on a small platform between the runners of the sleigh as he drove the horses. The church was lighted with tall candles, and all voices joined in the majestic Swedish hymn, "All hail to thee, O blessed morn." The joys of Christmas continued for a week.

But whatever the background, whatever the native rituals, whatever the customs of the celebration, on Christmas the magic of the season captured everyone.

49

Iowa

The first automobiles and buses were the beginning of the end for bobsleds. And yet, as these vehicles labored along the snow-packed, icy roads on narrow tires with their mechanical horsepower, they were sometimes passed by a neighbor's horses demonstrating "two-horse power" at ultimate speed. And in spite of the excitement of the new invention, it took time to exchange the joy of lying under buffalo robes on a bed of straw, for sitting upright on crowded, narrow seats.

But the practice of going to the country to visit grandparents continued, of course. Often the family went for the Christmas Eve celebration and stayed through Christmas Day.

When Grandfather clicked the catch that released the parlor doors on Christmas Eve, the air seemed electrified as everyone viewed the Christmas tree casting its age-old, ever-new splendor over everything in the familiar room. Walnuts covered with tinfoil hung from its green branches. Strings of popcorn and cran-

berries and kernels of red corn were festooned among the branches on which lighted candles burned. Shining red apples hung from sturdier branches. And always, gracing the highest branch that sometimes reached the ceiling, was the family's special, shining star.

Grandfather read the Christmas story, and at last the time came for the tree to yield its mysterious packages. Wrappings were torn off excitedly, and the rigid dignity of the parlor changed to delightful disorder. Grandfather's gift was the most unique—a footwarmer. "Fill with three quarts of boiling water. It can't roll over and it won't leak," the directions said. A marvelous invention!

The children played in the barn the next afternoon, loving the snorts and grunts and mutterings of the animals, while the yowling cats waited for a saucer of milk. On the ride home, the woods were dark against the far reaches of snow. But lights of other homesteads sparkled out their signals of joy.

North Dakota

Their homes were sod huts. Often they were built into a slight depression, like small fortresses made snug and sturdy against the prairie's winter winds. The tops of the huts were covered with sod too, as had been done in Scandinavia to add to their warmth. Cold nights drew the family, including the pet cat and dog, close to the fire crackling on the hearth. They had learned what to expect when a severe storm approached these treeless, remote areas. Snow fell thickly, and the biting winds increased. Novelist O. E. Rölvaag wrote descriptively of these days: "Blizzard after blizzard whipped heaven and earth into a milling whiteness. . . ."

But often after the harshest of storms, Christmas morn dawned clear, though bitter cold. The neighbors, whether relatives or friends, piled into their bobsled to join the nearest family. Sometimes farms were so far apart that get-togethers, especially in winter, were scarce. But sharing Christmas was a special, counted-on delight. Like latter-day Magi, those who came brought gifts, though at best humble and lowly.

The people were poor. But poverty never precluded the possibility of a beautiful Christmas. If possible a worship service was held in the schoolhouse on Christmas Day, the pastor wearing a black robe and a white ruff. Homes were decorated when paint buckets appeared and paper was brightly colored, then cut into yards of strips to festoon the room, or turned into cornucopias and filled with homemade candy, or into huge bells to hang in doorways. Godparents living close enough would visit the children, snuggle them in their laps, and tell joy-filled stories of other Christmases in other lands.

Dusk came early. The family was alone again, recounting memories of the day. Clear skies showed the immeasurable expanse of the heavens and the countless stars. And the wooden windmill, built close to the hut, stood as a silent sentinel keeping watch over all.

51

Wisconsin

Christmas Day! And all the family gathered for the day's activities. In the early country quiet the grandparents waited expectantly for sons and daughters, grandchildren, and aunts and uncles to arrive. They all attended the Christmas morning service at church; they enjoyed a sumptuous Christmas dinner; gifts piled under the tree were opened in the afternoon; and at dusk, grandfather, wearing his warm Norwegian sweater and a red wool cap, took the children for a ride on his horse-drawn sled.

Quickly they settled down on a bed of golden straw. They felt close to the animals as the cat settled down in granddaughter's lap, and the dog joined the merry group. They felt close to the land, and they knew the delight of riding on newfallen snow. The smell of wood smoke filled the air, and snow-laced trees sighed and swayed and beckoned them on. Over a smooth stretch of road, the children saw grandfather clutch the reins firmly and heard his "Eh-yup" to the horses

as he settled them into a smart trot; they heard the harness bells chime a gentle song as their voices, too, shouted with joy!

Later, when fond good-byes had been said, each family left for home savoring memories of the day. Grandmother's kitchen, plainly the biggest and best room in the house, was the heart of the home. They thought of their large family gathered around the table: they recalled the tantalizing aroma of roast goose; bread baked that very morning; vegetables of four varieties; preserves of wild grapes, crabapples, and wild blackberries. And always the traditional Christmas cookies. It had not been hard to thank God for his abundance as they had eaten in grandmother's kitchen. Their hearts warmed again at the memory of the wood crackling quietly on the hearth.

Pale white stars lit the sky, and sighing winds whispered again to each of them: "It is Christmas! Christmas! Christ is born!"

Illinois

The scene was like a Christmas card picture of a typical afternoon in the Yuletide season. The train was late, but at three o'clock Number 123 pulled into the station at Centerville, Illinois, and the station platform, crowded with those who eagerly waited, were united with relatives and friends who came to meet them. Sleighs and bobsleds and a few of those newfangled automobiles would take them to their destinations for the celebration of Christmas.

On the way, everyone was bursting with questions. What was it like—riding in a train? How was grandfather who was too weak to make the trip? How were their friends and neighbors who lived nearby? How had the crops been? How did they like the new young pastor who had been with them the past few months? Question after question, report after report, and then the "Whoa, whoa" to the horses, or the clattering new car coming to a faltering stop, announced their arrival to those who had waited at home.

Perhaps their Christmases were not as elaborate as ours today. But there were church services, concerts, family traditions that originated in other homelands, sharing of Christmas baking, and Christmas trees trimmed with strings of popcorn and colored cutouts, and always, shining in their darkened rooms, the lighted candles. Sometimes they sang their Christmas songs until midnight, perhaps with no artistic triumph, but with a sentiment expressed that was wholly sincere, and a spontaneous spirit that we sometimes miss today. It was a shining Christmas!

These people observed Christmas not merely for the moment. It was for them a storehouse of love and faith and hope for the long winter ahead. And their patience, and perseverance, and ingenuity still shine brightly, helping to light our way. For of all the gifts they gave us, the greatest was perhaps the gift given from their hearts: the knowledge of their faith in God whose Son was born in a manger in Bethlehem.

Arizona

Christmas also came to the White Mountains in Arizona. Wood was stacked high by the log house for the hearth fire, and father and son came from a nearby wooded area triumphantly bearing the tree. Christmas Eve was celebrated with considerable magnificence. It was for everyone!

Often, nearby Indian missions announced a midnight service as bells rang out. They had prepared a crib for the Christ child, and the figure was carried to the high altar and placed above the tabernacle. A choir of voices intoned the Kyrie in Latin, and, although most of the worshipers did not understand the words, their responses showed that they understood the spirit of the blessed night. As the Indians left, each one in the long line paused to take a turn at swinging the crib. After the service, everyone enjoyed tamales. Each year one of the families was honored by being chosen to make them.

Mexicans joined in the festivities too, performing plays and with troubadour singing. The plaintive tones of the singers and the simplicity of the people brought the imaginations of some of the observers back to the Middle Ages. In their impromptu ballads there was always a twinge of ancient romance. Boxes containing various dainties were opened, and everyone joined in their contribution to the Christmas feast.

Christmas had come again to the White Mountains in Arizona. The combination of woods and valleys and mountains must have awakened feelings of gratitude to their Creator for all these gifts. And now they gave thanks for his Son. They had honored him with the ritual of the swinging crib. They had performed their plays, and their lyric songs had sung his praise. They had celebrated his coming throughout the night, and as morning dawned they saw a wisp of gloriously shining white cloud caught on the peak of a near mountain!

54

St. Olaf College, Northfield, Minnesota

Christmas Festival at St. Olaf

LOIS RAND

MANITOU HEIGHTS glistens as amber lights reflect on frost and snow. A sharp, cold wind buffets the crowds hurrying along paths and roadways in the crisp December night. Anticipation quickens as they stream toward the auditorium to experience together a great first act in the year's observance of Christmas.

This is a familiar scene on the campus of St. Olaf College in Northfield, Minnesota, as the college community and visitors share again the wonder of the holy season the first weekend in December.

Similar scenes occur across the land in the weeks before Christmas. Traditions become entwined with specific places and events as people seek to clothe the celebration of the incarnation in appropriately shining garments. How can it be that an event so personal, so quiet and so self-effacing as the first Christmas in the stable of Bethlehem can be faithfully honored in forms and settings so magnified, multiplied, and publicized?

The Christmas celebration at St. Olaf suggests an answer. Over 4000 persons wedge themselves into every available seat each of the three nights the

Olaf Christiansen

F. Melius Christiansen

Christmas festival is given. Another 2500 have been unsuccessful in obtaining the free but much-sought tickets. Approximately 500 students join to make the great story audible and visible in their individual choirs, as a combined chorus, and *en masse* with the audience.

The lights dim; dancers move from the shadows in a swirl of color as they set the mood. Music flows from carol to chorale to lullaby to anthem and back again, uninterrupted by announcement. The audience sits hushed and enthralled, breaking out in song at three or four points as programmed, almost as a relief from emotional intensity. The music evokes not only nostalgia and a sense of beauty, but also a lifting of the heart at the nobility and grandeur of the old, simple story. The spirit of the first Christmas permeates, just as it surely enfolded the little group around the manger.

This is an event of the Babe, not of the choirs. It becomes not a concert, but a true festival. Music carefully chosen, lovingly prepared, beautifully rendered, and gratefully heard is as suitable a vehicle as there can be for regenerating the adoration first felt by the shepherds at Bethlehem.

The 1980 festival is the 69th in the history of this Lutheran, liberal arts college. As those years have passed, the festival has evolved in response to the times, but it has not wavered from its first intention to be a song service preparing the St. Olaf community

for a true and significant celebration of Christmastide.

That intention was conceived and put into action by Dr. F. Melius Christiansen, the founder of the St. Olaf Choir and for years the leader of musical life and experience at the college. He planned the first such service to be conducted December 17, 1912, for the 334 students before they scattered to their homes for Christmas vacation. The St. Olaf Choral Union, as the chorus was listed in the program, was augmented by tenor and violin soloists, a quartet, and a speaker, the Rev. R. M. Fjeldstad, a recently-ordained St. Olaf graduate.

From the beginning of this venture, Christiansen had a close ally and collaborator in P. G. Schmidt, a fellow faculty member who in 1912 was college vice-president and treasurer, and for many years was manager of the band and the choir. Together they worked out the details for those early Christmas services. Each year, Christiansen conceived the idea, wrote music and trained singers; Schmidt arranged programs, seating, lighting, ushers, promotion, and the countless other details that enabled the music to be performed and appreciated . . . and then he sang bass with the choir. The teamwork of those two continued until their retirements in the 1940s and 1950s, when they gradually turned their work over to their sons, Olaf C. Christiansen and Frederick A. Schmidt.

F. Melius Christiansen's skill as a conductor and composer made a permanent impact on this event and established a pattern of using a wide array of music.

Bach and other old masters have always been included, as have contemporary composers. Many cultures have contributed folk music. But there has been another truly unique element: Christiansen composed and arranged an amazing number of choral works tailor-made for the pure *a cappella* sound he and his choirs made famous. Many of these works were written especially for these Christmas festivals and have since been used extensively by numerous other choirs. "Today There Is Ringing," "This Night," "Lullaby on Christmas Eve," and the perennial St. Olaf favorite, "Beautiful Savior," are among the best known and most loved. The two successors to Christiansen, his son Olaf and Dr. Kenneth Jennings, have continued to include selections from his works as well as compositions of their own and of other faculty members and former students.

Through the years, many other music specialists have added their skills to help develop this significant occasion into an event of increasing beauty and impact. In the early 1920s, the music department added a faculty member whose contributions for over 25 years enriched the content and cemented the tradition of this service. Oscar Overby directed the Ladies Chorus, wrote texts for numerous Christiansen compositions, and gave abundant energy to the difficult task of preparing the massed choirs—a function the planners held to be of highest importance. As the number of musicians grew larger, he devised the most workable methods of staging them and gave attention to possible improvements each year.

Programs on which he made notes as guides for the following year show that no detail was too small for his attention: "Use as few ligh   ssible." "Use more drama." "Prophecy very eff   "Plan ventilation so no usher goes around an   rbs the program." "The first choir singing 'Beau   Savior' in the basement was not heard." And he   e precise notes and charts on seating arrangements   rom such respect for detail comes the polish and effectiveness that allows the musicianship freedom to soar. Overby was a remarkable blend of the creative and the pragmatic, and was the ideal complement to the impressive talents of Christiansen and Schmidt. Olaf recalls, "Overby was a real dreamer, full of ideas and so fertile. Often my dad would write music and hand it to Oscar who would then write words. He wrote texts for about half my dad's anthems."

It is impossible to think of Overby's contributions without thinking also of Gertrude Boe, a St. Olaf music student who married Overby shortly after her graduation in 1923. Her clear soprano was already beloved by F. Melius and by audiences during her student days; she was to continue for many years in this role as well as teaching voice at the college. There are still many who cannot think of the Christmas festivals of earlier days without hearing her lovely voice singing the solos in "Beautiful Savior" and "Lullaby on Christmas Eve." Christiansen had been entranced with the Norwegian *"Vuggesang"* ("Cradle Song") and had arranged it as a solo. In late 1934, a few days before the festival, Overby was at home with an attack of flu and a high fever when F. Melius phoned and excitedly played and sang his idea for a choral version of *"Vuggesang."* He requested an immediate set of English words to use in the coming festival. Flu and all, Overby

Oscar and Gertrude Overby

Kenneth Jennings and Donald Berglund

wrote the words, c[...]ere made of the arrangement, and "Lullaby[...]ristmas Eve" was in rehearsal the next day w[...]ertrude Boe Overby as the soloist. Shortly befo[...]r death in 1979 she was still smiling at that mem[...]ble spurt of creativity.

These colleagues [...]de the most of each opportunity, and, when necessary, even of misfortune. When Hoyme Chapel was destroyed by fire in 1923, the Christmas festival was moved to the gymnasium, where its planners faced new challenges and readily devised new solutions, finding in the gym a chance to inject new drama into the service.

Early each fall when the festival planning committee met, they grappled with creative concepts often suggested, explained, and rapidly sketched on the blackboard by Arnold Flaten of the art department. John Berntson, the meticulous, beauty-loving grounds manager, would scarcely hear the entire concept before he was finding some ingenious means to solve the staging problems. Schmidt was busily plotting the support functions, while Christiansen and Overby fairly oozed musical ideas that would combine to make a memorable whole.

Thousands still recall occasions during the 44 years the old gym housed the festival when choir singers robed in white descended improvised stairs from the running track, singing, "From heaven above to earth I come." They remember Gertrude Boe Overby's voice like a single golden thread spinning its way from somewhere up under the roof, "This little child of lowly birth shall be the joy of all the earth," and, floating back from another secret corner, a contralto echo, ". . . of all the earth." And they speak of manger scenes with angels and shepherds, and sometimes faculty children coming to peer down at a real baby. Those particular features have been lost due to the increased size of the event, but they are warmly remembered.

When Dr. Olaf Christiansen arrived in 1941 to take up the reins his father had held so long, he brought with him memories from his Northfield childhood and his student days at the college, as well as a clear understanding of the festi-

Alice Larsen

val's purpose. But he was an innovator too, willing to try new approaches and more drama in order to move the larger and larger audiences to an intimate experience.

A particular characteristic of his father's programming had become a traditional ending for the evening. A ladies' quartet, hidden from view, sang a haunting Christiansen arrangement of "Silent Night," often as the

figure of an angel robed in white appeared at the top of the stairs. Olaf tried a change. "Beautiful Savior" previously had quite regularly been sung somewhere in the program; he often used only the last phrases of it as an equally effective ending.

Insistent as these men have been on quality, neither of the Christiansens nor Jennings have let themselves be bound fast to a rigid programming habit. They have preferred to explore occasional change, striking a happy balance between custom and freshness. In their individual ways, their aim has been to convey the pure message and childlike spirit of the music. Olaf recalls as a youth seeing his father sometimes weep for joy while conducting; later, he found himself doing the same thing as the youthful conviction of the singers swept over him, and caught and gripped the listeners.

To find each year a new way to tell the same story is not easy, as every pastor and Sunday school program director has discovered. In the early festival song services, there was no attempt at a theme beyond the general nature of the Christmas story itself and humanity's response to it. Although music was the primary vehicle, the Christmas gospel was always read, and until 1933 there was usually an address by a noted guest pastor or church official. During the presidency of Lars W. Boe in the 1920s and 1930s, it was his custom to read the gospel and bring a greeting. Texts of prophecy were sometimes added, and eventually only the selected scripture texts were used, interspersed in relation to the music.

In 1938, the printed program carried the title, "The Morning Star," the first indication of a specific festival theme. Each year since then, a particular thought has been chosen to provide a central focus around which the music revolves. "How Shall I Receive Thee," "From Darkness into Light," "We Beheld His Glory," "Wonder Anew," and many others have been used and occasionally reused.

"Wonder Anew," the theme for the 1975 festival, was a happy accident. An old copy of the F. Melius Christiansen anthem, "Praise to the Lord," which includes the sentence, "Ponder anew what the Almighty can do," had been misprinted, "Wonder anew." Though the copy had been corrected in subsequent publications, Dr. Jennings, the 1968 successor to Olaf Christiansen, felt the error contained a great thought worthy of emphasis. From this misprint came one of the most poignant of all the festival themes.

As the years have passed, the choral

Robert Scholz

"Wonder anew . . ."

groups have grown from one or two to three, four, and finally five. Other faculty and student directors have come and gone, sharing the responsibilities of preparing and conducting the constantly changing crop of student musicians. Together, they have made tremendous contributions to the structure begun by the founders. The number of participating students has increased from about 50 to nearly 500 today, consistently 18 to 20 percent of the student body.

Finding space for musicians and listeners is always a problem. In 1967, when the new Skoglund complex increased the seating capacity from the old gym's 2000 to over 4000, the festival schedule was decreased to three nights from the four it had been for several years. (This was a relief to professors in other departments who had been expressing concern over the heavy demands of time and energy just before exams!) But the additional space was filled immediately.

Donald Sahling, director of public functions, says that dealing with the ticket requests is easily the biggest headache of his year. A block of tickets is set aside for students. Request envelopes from alumni, parents, friends, and strangers—nearly all postmarked the stipulated date of October 1—spill from stuffed mail bags onto his office floor. Each year he receives at least 2500 more requests than he can fill. But even handling that often thankless job, where he fields the criticisms that come no matter how fair and efficient the system, Sahling says the satisfactions of working with this event far outweigh the complications.

Sahling does have the convenience of computerized ticket numbering. Until a decade ago, Fred Schmidt and his father before him numbered the row and seat on each ticket by hand—and alone. One year Schmidt and his secretary tried to share the task. Somehow, one row was numbered twice, and the resulting furor eliminated that approach forever.

Today Sahling and his battalion of ushers somehow direct to their seats in reasonably short order the fortunate ticket holders and always some walk-ins who benefit by the inevitable few who have tickets but do not appear. A special audience of several hundred is welcomed to the Thursday evening dress rehearsal. This has traditionally been a time to invite residents of retirement homes and institutions for the handicapped in the area. They hear and see nearly everything in more comfort than if they were part of the crush on Friday, Saturday, and Sunday evenings. And they may enjoy some extras. All the participants would agree that the dress rehearsal is a tense, complicated effort to put together a mass of intricate bits into a smooth whole. As Olaf Christiansen commented, "To do it requires good will among men, but it's exciting, too."

Each night, the front of Skoglund auditorium's large space is filled to overflowing with the Manitou Singers (freshmen women directed by Alice T. Larsen), Viking Chorus (freshmen men directed by Dr. Robert Scholz), the Campus and Chapel Choirs (also directed by Dr. Scholz), and the St. Olaf Choir directed by Dr. Jennings, who must ultimately coordinate the activity. Between these groups and the audience sits the 80-piece St. Olaf Orchestra, directed by David O'Dell.

Instrumentalists have complemented the vocalists in some way most years. After the loss of the organ in the Hoyme Chapel fire and the move to a gymnasium setting, instrumental ensembles grew gradually in importance and size. They add to the beauty of the processional and recessional, accompany the audience in carol singing, and occasionally combine with the choirs for a special work. Beatrix Lien, who taught violin at the college during her entire career, recalls leading the carol singing with her violin bow from her place as then director and concertmistress of the fledgling orchestra. With the arrival of Dr. Donald Berglund as orchestra director in 1946, the orchestra assumed a steadily stronger role. The faithful and gifted musicianship of Dr. Berglund and Miss Lien through several decades until the late 1970s is evident today in an orchestra whose fine symphonic quality is the perfect foil for the *a cappella* singing which is still the core of the festival.

The audience singing has been led for years by Dr. Berglund, succeeded now by Mr. O'Dell. Among other favorites, the Norwegian *"Jeg Er Så Glad Hver Julekveld"* ("How glad I am each Christmas Eve") is nearly always sung in the original Norwegian not only by old hands at it, but also by those who stumble over the language but find strength in numbers.

An interesting frame always surrounds the musicians and underscores the theme. There are Susan Bauer's dancers, using any available sliver of space to set the theme in motion. There is an array of Christmas trees, perhaps a set of Christmas pictures projected on the front walls or glittering stars suspended from the ceiling, and banners set in place during the winding processional through the audience. These visual feasts usually are the fruit in large measure of art teachers John Maakestad and Arch Leean and their assistants.

At the lighting control center sits college electrician

59

Perry Kruse, who has been creating these lighting effects since he was a student in the mid-1960s. His crew of six students responds to his intricate cue sheets and directions, using a mix of spotlights, color effects, and darkness to enhance the music and involve the audience more personally in the mood. Kruse says his volunteers are so committed to this task that they often come back to assist in some way even after graduation. Their work is all done in three set-up and rehearsal nights and three festival nights, but they log nearly 250 hours during that time. Their biggest challenge came in 1975 when the Jerome Foundation funded the televising of the festival for distribution through the Public Broadcasting System. The light crew had an instant lesson in television production while the Twin Cities' channel 2 television personnel had a comparable learning experience as they confronted the size and purpose of this undertaking.

Televising the festival was equally stressful for the musicians who were required to give attention to details outside their usual purview, and found it hard to concentrate as they usually do on the business at hand. However, the effort was successful, and "Wonder Anew" has been rerun each December since 1975 by many public television stations across the United States, on the armed services network overseas, and recently also in Norway.

Every year's festival weekend requires a tremendous support system if the efforts of the festival participants are to be effective. Who will coordinate the invasion of the physical education department and set up the seating? Will food service director Mike Simione, with his Italian background, manage to produce another authentic Norwegian smorgasbord each night? Who will prepare and serve it to the hundreds of lutefisk and lefse devotees? If there is a snowfall, will the walks and roads be shovelled in time? Where can all those extra cars be parked, and who will direct the traffic snarl when so many people try to depart at once? Are there hosts and hostesses at all strategic spots? Can Skoglund and the St. Olaf Center be cleaned and re-arranged in time for the next crowd? Will the programs be accurate and back from the printer in time? Who will select and set up the Christmas tree? How will John Maakestad get the stars hung from the ceiling?

Providing consistent answers to questions such as these involves detailed planning and follow-through by an army of maintenance, food service, faculty, staff, and student personnel. Most of them are never seen nor heard by the visitors, but without their help the festival would be crippled as surely as if an epidemic struck the musicians.

Despite the most meticulous preparations in all quarters, there is still an occasional hitch. Such incidents are recalled afterward with chuckles, when the passing of time has dimmed the momentary anxiety.

There was the young man who was listening from the running track in the old gym when he fainted and fell to the floor below. He was rescued by Fred Schmidt, crawling on hands and knees to pull him out.

There was the second row of Manitou Singers who once mistakenly occupied one riser too high, and those behind them followed their lead. When the choirs sat, there was an open space behind row one, and the last row of girls sat on the laps of the boys behind them, accompanied by stifled giggling.

There was the gentleman who one year sent President Sidney Rand a long, testy letter after the night he had attended. He hadn't liked his seats; he thought the orchestra had been out of tune; the gym was too hot and crowded; and, to complete his indignation, his wife had snagged and ruined her hose on a rough seat. The president replied in as sympathetic a fashion as possible, offering also to reimburse the man's wife for the cost of the stockings. In due course a second, very short letter arrived, in which the gentleman acknowledged, "My wife told me I should never have sent that first letter."

These are the infrequent bits of ash that fall occasionally with the stardust. They are mostly remarkable for their scarcity. A persistent glow is far more noticeable. It is reflected in the words of a student singer, "It's so much work, but it's all worth it. There's no way to describe the joy of being surrounded by that heavenly music. It does seem heavenly, even if we're singing."

If that student should ever return as part of the audience, she may feel yet another thrill. Gertrude Overby, after enjoying the festival in retirement, said, "It seems so worshipful and uplifting now. It always was wonderful, but there were always so many cues and instructions to remember years ago." Yet at that very time, countless others were feeling exactly what she felt later in the audience, beneficiaries of her devoted attention to responsibility.

The program lists no credits, and has not for many years. Dr. Jennings, who was a student at St. Olaf under Olaf Christiansen, reflected on their mutual feeling: "We try always to be on guard against commercialization. We don't want this to be presented for personal credit; we'd rather take the program space to print the texts for the music. We want to say something about Christmas very beautifully and help prepare people for Christmas."

The question: Can something so complex and finite be a fit vehicle to honor someone so simple and yet eternal? The answer, on the St. Olaf campus and surely many other places: Yes. The secret is the unswerving commitment to see the Babe, to adore him, to reflect him. With that underpinning, relentless change, unsettling problems, occasional disgruntled individuals, even success and popularity can be absorbed without damage. A festival such as this can remain alive, vigorous, responsive, and faithful to the Lord it honors.

Christmas Has a Secret

MICHAEL DRURY

THERE IS an old legend about Christmas bread that I cherish. It goes something like this: Anything given to others at Christmastime is holy bread; the act of dividing it multiplies it. At Christmas, one loaf would be enough to feed the whole world. I believe that legend, for I have seen it happen—most recently last year.

I had spent months writing a book that I deeply believed in and I had become temporarily poor in the process. I had planned to scrape along on savings, but a book always takes longer than you expect. There are also stretches when you are sure that the work is no good and that you must have been mad to attempt it. I was in such a spell as Christmas drew near. There was little I could do to make merry except send a few cards.

Then I received a card from someone 3000 miles away, with a check for five dollars enclosed. Three years earlier I had given this friend five dollars in a small emergency. Now she was able to return it and did so gladly. I'm not really one for "signs and wonders," but that little check lay on my worktable for days, curiously spurring my faith in the work I was doing.

There is a man who has been kind to me, and I had hoped to buy him a book that cost $5.95. I had already discarded this idea because I couldn't afford it; now I could squeak it out. But was that practical? I rather needed that five dollars, and the man wouldn't expect a gift; we weren't on that sort of basis. Yet the complete surprise of it was part of the pleasure—and any-

way, there was the matter of holy bread. I bought the book and wrapped it in bright paper. I felt immensely happy every time I looked at it.

Two days later another greeting card arrived with a 10 dollar bill folded into it—in appreciation of a small service I had once performed for a neighbor. "Christmas bread!" I thought. "It really does multiply." Then I heard of a young couple in great financial difficulty, and I sent the 10 dollars to them. I wasn't actually poor or hungry, and I knew what an unexpected boost can mean far beyond its cash value. After all, I had just received two of them myself. It was Christmas bread. It had watered my soul; now it was time to pass it on.

On the afternoon before Christmas I sat down with a cup of tea and a piece of fruitcake and began opening the day's mail. In a letter from my sister was a check for 100 dollars. She knew of my book, and it was her way of saying, "Keep on." I sat looking at it for a full minute. A bit later I tore open a letter from a bank and learned that a loan had been repaid to my mother's estate—enough for me to live on for several months. I could now finish my job with ease. Holy bread, indeed. When you share it, you cannot get rid of the stuff. How can I not believe the old story? Legends become legends because they are rooted in deep laws of life.

Our family used to know an old woman on a California ranch who would ask people, "How do you keep Christmas?" As a child I found that funny—as if you kept Christmas in a cedar chest, salted it down in the meat locker, or tied it up in the corral. But now I know how perfectly exact that expression is. Christmas does have to be kept. If it is not, it simply vanishes.

There are always some, of course, who cannot keep Christmas—and others who help. My mother and grandmother were invariably aware of those they called down-and-outers. I have seen them put a quarter into the Salvation Army kettle when it was half of all they had themselves. They took supplies to a cellar on the waterfront where an old sailor cooked a Christmas dinner of sorts for derelicts and loners like himself. I say "of sorts" because the menu was beef stew and unbuttered Italian bread, with apples and oranges for dessert. It was tasty and plentiful, though, and there was an open fire where a person could sit all afternoon if he wished.

But there is another group of people who will not keep Christmas, and they are increasing at an alarming rate. These are not the lonely and lost, but the successful, the middle-to-rich financially who often have families and many friends. They moan about boredom, expense, the rat race, phoniness, and fraud—and they do it with a strange pride. It has become almost chic to be anti-Christmas.

Last year somebody said to me aloud and without apology: "I hate Christmas! I wish the government would ban it, like DDT." More and more newspapers run December articles about yuletide depression. Suicides go up. Psychologists on radio and television discuss holiday gloom and offer palliatives.

And all the while they are hungry for Christmas bread. The scorners boast of maturity and sophistication, but actually they're indulging in a childish yen for a time when somebody else took responsibility for creating mystery and delight. How do they think it happened, except that someone standing where they now are standing made the effort?

Outside a village church in Switzerland one cold winter night a tired man waited for the evening service to begin. He had come a long way, and the church was dark. He began to wonder if any service was planned—despite the ringing of the bells that had lured him there.

But then through the forest he saw pinpricks of light bobbing and moving toward him. The congregation was assembling, each group carrying its own lighted lantern. After a few had arrived, the weary man followed them and sank down on a pew in the shadowy church. As more and more people came, each hanging his lantern on an iron hook in the wall, the shadows retreated and the church began to glow with light.

After the service the traveler stopped to ask the pastor about this unique method of illuminating the church.

"But it is the only means we have, *monsieur*," the clergyman replied. "In the 1500s when many of these churches were built, it was too costly for the church to supply candles. It was usual for each family to carry a lantern. Our church has chosen to carry on the old custom. If someone does not come, we all feel it. The church is darker by one lantern." He paused and looked sharply at the visitor. Then he added, "We are called the Church of the Lighted Lamps."

The traveler thanked his host and went away, knowing at last what he must do to regain his joy in living. He had to carry his own lamp.

In the 30 or 40 years since I first heard it, that story has more than once rekindled my own lantern. Last year I could not stand it any longer: I had to know if it was true. I wrote to a total stranger in Switzerland, a clergyman and editor. He replied that the story was true—though, of course, he could not vouch for the traveler. He said the village churches are electrified now, but a few were not yet electrified in the 1930s and 1940s; the iron hooks can still be seen in the walls.

Christmas is good only because we make it good—for no other reason. That is part of its message. There is much we can do for ourselves, and much we must do. In the dark night when the earth sleeps, Christmas trees bloom with light and color; the crisp air is scented with hearth fires and spices; houses are polished and decorated; bells ring; voices are raised in laughter and hymns; people salute one another and exchange beribboned packages—all because human beings make it so. Nature does this sort of thing the rest of the year; at Christmastime it's up to us.

It is not always easy. There are many times when an adult's eyes shine not with wonder but with tears. Yet tears refract and multiply light. The assertion of the spirit against odds is exactly what makes human beings human, different from other creatures. If you complain about it, there is no way the Spirit can come to you as it came to Mary long ago. But take whatever fragment you can and divide it—and joy will stream back upon you.

Do at least one totally unselfish thing for someone, even if he or she doesn't deserve it—perhaps *especially* if he doesn't. Take a supermarket poinsettia (rather inexpensive) to that tiresome neighbor or the couple in the next block you usually avoid. Invite just one person over for coffee and cookies, if that's all the time or money you can spare. But if you can afford more, put on a party for children in a hospital, old people at a center, those who have to work on Christmas Day—firemen, police, switchboard operators at hospitals or hotels. And don't just send something; go there yourself. It isn't just the poor who need you. Do something for a rich friend; they suffer too.

Create at least one spot of beauty. Spend a dollar or two for something decorative—a bunch of greens, a pair of bayberry candles, a box of gleaming ornaments —and arrange it in your living quarters. Make a paper chain the way you did at school—aluminum foil and cellophane tape will do nicely—and loop it in front of a mirror or crisscross it over a window.

It may sound absurd to say that anything so public as Christmas has a secret, but it does and this is it: It is necessary to light your own lantern in the darkness. The customs must be kept—guarded and cared for—if Christmas is to take on life for us. The bread is offered, but it has to be eaten—and shared.

Randolph E. Haugan

OVER 50 years ago, a dream stirred Randolph Haugan; a dream that he hoped one day would be expressed in a book about Christmas.

Employed by Augsburg Publishing House directly after graduation from college in 1924, Haugan was soon named its general manager. Along with the rigorous demands of this position, he spent time ferreting out possibilities for his dream, weighing the problems it posed against the urgency of the message of the Christmas miracle. Little by little the rough edges of his plan became smooth, and at last the pattern was defined and clearly discernible.

Five decades later, with the publication of this issue, Editor Haugan has edited 50 volumes of a much-loved Christmas annual. And for a host of readers, it is the harbinger each year of the Christmas season.

Today, *Christmas* appears regularly on seasonal best-seller lists, and in the years since volume 1 came off the presses in 1931, approximately five million copies of the annual have been printed. It was not always a success story in the publishing trade, however. Introduced during the Depression, the first edition of 5000 copies had an uncertain market, as did the next edition, and the next. But even with nagging doubts, Haugan pursued his dream undaunted—the telling of the old, ever-new Christmas story through music, art, and literature. As the years passed, *Christmas* was taken to the hearts of more readers until for many families it has now become an American tradition.

For Haugan, memories of Christmas go back to childhood days in rural Wisconsin. In his home, his church (where his father was the pastor), and his community, the season was observed reverently and was filled with the mystery of joy and wonder. His Norwegian immigrant parents brought customs from their native land which have been woven into the pages of *Christmas* together with traditions from around the world. The focus of the publication has always been on the religious significance of the season.

In 1970, Haugan retired as general manager of Augsburg Publishing House. He continued, however, to serve as editor of *Christmas* in his retirement.

When Haugan planned this, his last edition of *Christmas*, he was as exuberant and as magnificently curious as he was for the first edition, his sense of perennial discovery just as vital. And always, with a master editor's intrigue, he transferred his marvelous sense of excitement to his co-workers.

He gave much in the process of fulfilling his dream, and he asked much. And in the giving and the asking the dream became a reality. For through 50 years, *Christmas* brought the good news of Christ's birth to unnumbered hearts who heard and treasured the message of the angel: "Unto you is born this night . . . a Savior!"

MELVA ROREM

The greatest event in history was the coming of the Christ child. For the past 50 years, we have attempted to glorify God and to remind us all of this event through music, literature, and art.

This is the last volume of Christmas *for which I will be responsible. I would like to thank the artists, writers, composers, and craftsmen who have contributed their many talents to make this publication possible.*

RANDOLPH E. HAUGAN, EDITOR

Volume I - 1931

Volume II - 1932

Volume III - 1933

Volume IV - 1934

Volume V - 1935

Volume VI - 1936

Volume VII - 1937

Volume VIII - 1938

Volume IX - 1939

Volume X - 1940

Volume XI - 1941

Volume XII - 1942

Volume XIII - 1943

Volume XIV - 1944

Volume XV - 1945

Volume XVI - 1946

Volume XVII - 1947

Volume XVIII - 1948

Volume XIX - 1949

Volume XX - 1950

Volume XXI - 1951

Volume XXII - 1952

Volume XXIII - 1953

Volume XXIV - 1954

Volumé XXV - 1955

Volume XXVI -1956

Volume XXVII - 1957

Volume XXVIII - 1958

Volume XXIX - 1959

Volume XXX - 1960

Volume XXXI - 1961

Volume XXXII - 1962

Volume XXXIII - 1963

Volume XXXIV - 1964

Volume. XXXV - 1965

Volume XXXVI - 1966

Volume XXXVII - 1967

Volume XXXVIII - 1968

Volume XXXIX - 1969

Volume XL - 1970

Volume XLI - 1971

Volume XLII - 1972

Volume XLIII - 1973

Volume XLIV - 1974

Volume XLV - 1975

Volume XLVI - 1976

Volume XLVII —1977

Volume XLVIII —1978

Volume XLIX —1979